11+ Verbal Reasoning

For GL Assessment – ages 10-11

Preparing for the GL 11+ Verbal Reasoning test can feel like a real challenge... but fear not! This CGP book is stuffed to bursting with the best revision and practice around!

It's got plenty of revision notes, top tips and excellent examples, as well as questions that are sure to test your knowledge and polish your skills.

Just when you thought that was it, there are also mixed practice tests, two full practice papers, and answers for every question. You'll certainly be raring to go on the big day.

Complete
Revision & Practice

<u>Everything</u> you need to pass the test!

Contents

Section Four — Maths and Sequences

Section Five — Logic and Coding

Published by CGP

Editors:
Claire Boulter, Emma Cleasby, Rebecca Greaves and Rebecca Russell.

With thanks to Alex Fairer and Becca Lakin for the proofreading.

ISBN: 978 1 78908 601 0

Printed by Elanders Ltd, Newcastle upon Tyne.
Clipart from Corel®

What's in the 11+

Here's a quick overview of what's in the 11+ to help you get your head round the basics.

The **11+** is an **Admissions Test**

1) The 11+ is a test used by <u>some schools</u> to help with their <u>selection process</u>.

2) You'll usually take it when you're in <u>Year 6</u>, at some point during the <u>autumn term</u>.

3) Schools <u>use the results</u> to decide who to accept. They might also use <u>other things</u> to help make up their mind, like information about <u>where you live</u>.

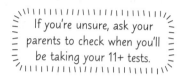

If you're unsure, ask your parents to check when you'll be taking your 11+ tests.

Some Schools test a **Mixture** of **Subjects**

1) There are <u>four</u> main subjects that can be tested in the 11+, so <u>depending</u> on the <u>school</u> you're applying for, you might sit papers on <u>some</u> or <u>all</u> of these:

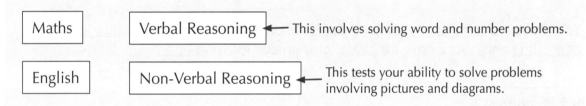

| Maths | Verbal Reasoning | ← This involves solving word and number problems. |

| English | Non-Verbal Reasoning | ← This tests your ability to solve problems involving pictures and diagrams. |

2) This book will help you with the <u>Verbal Reasoning</u> part of the test.

Get to **Know** what **Kind** of **Paper** you're taking

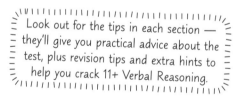

Look out for the tips in each section — they'll give you practical advice about the test, plus revision tips and extra hints to help you crack 11+ Verbal Reasoning.

Your paper will either be <u>multiple choice</u> or <u>standard answer</u>.

Multiple Choice

1) For each question you'll be given some <u>options</u> on a <u>separate answer sheet</u>.

2) You'll need to mark your answer with a clear pencil <u>line</u> in the box next to the <u>option</u> that you think is <u>correct</u>.

Standard Answer

1) You'll have to <u>write down</u> the correct answer for some questions, but you may have some <u>options</u> to choose from for others.

2) You'll usually <u>mark</u> or <u>write</u> your answer on the <u>question paper</u>.

Check which type of <u>question paper</u> you'll be taking, so you know what it <u>looks</u> like and <u>where</u> your answers go. Try to do some practice tests in the <u>same format</u> as the test you'll be taking, so you know what to <u>expect</u> on the day.

What's in the 11+ Verbal Reasoning Test

Get your brain ready for Verbal Reasoning by reading about the different question types.

Verbal Reasoning involves Solving Problems

1) Although you won't have <u>learnt</u> how to answer Verbal Reasoning questions <u>at school</u>, you've probably already <u>picked up</u> some of the <u>skills</u> you need for the test.

2) There are lots of different <u>question types</u> that can crop up.
We've grouped them into <u>categories</u>:

The Alphabet

You'll need to use the <u>alphabet</u> to answer these questions.
Knowing your alphabet <u>inside out</u> will really help you.

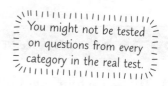

You might not be tested on questions from every category in the real test.

Making Words

You'll need to <u>form words</u> using other words or letters. You'll need a <u>good grasp of spelling</u> and how words are <u>made</u>, plus an eye for <u>spotting letter patterns</u>.

Word Meanings

These questions test your <u>vocabulary</u> and <u>word knowledge</u>. Questions of this type will ask you to think about the <u>meanings of words</u> or find <u>connections</u> between them.

Maths and Sequences

You'll need to show that you can <u>work with numbers</u>. Make sure your <u>mental maths</u> is up to scratch, as well as your <u>times tables</u> and <u>basic maths skills</u>. For sequence questions, you'll need to spot <u>letter</u> or <u>number patterns</u> and find the <u>next step</u>.

Logic and Coding

For logic questions, you'll need to show that you <u>understand information</u> and can pick out the <u>key points</u>. Coding questions will test your <u>maths</u> and <u>logic skills</u>, as well as your ability to spot <u>rules</u> and <u>complete patterns</u>.

3) Certain <u>question types</u> in these categories come up more <u>often</u> than others in the test.

4) We've labelled these questions as '<u>Key Examples</u>' in this book to show you which are the most <u>important</u> question types.

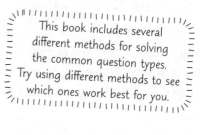

This book includes several different methods for solving the common question types. Try using different methods to see which ones work best for you.

5) This <u>doesn't</u> mean you should ignore the rest —
it's just to show you which questions to <u>focus</u> on,
especially if you're <u>pushed for time</u>.

How to Prepare for the 11+

Give yourself a head start with your Verbal Reasoning preparation — be organised and plan ahead.

Divide your Preparation into Stages

1) You should find a way to prepare for the 11+ that suits you. This may depend on how much time you have before the test. Here's a good way to plan your Verbal Reasoning revision:

> Use this book to revise strategies for answering different question types. Read through the study notes and follow the worked examples carefully — make sure you understand the method used at each step.

↓

> Do plenty of practice questions, concentrating on the question types you find tricky.

↓

> Sit some practice papers to prepare yourself for the real test.

2) When you first start answering Verbal Reasoning questions, try to solve the questions without making any mistakes, rather than working quickly.

3) Once you feel confident about the questions, then you can build up your speed.

4) You can do this by asking an adult to time you as you answer a set of questions, or by seeing how many questions you can answer in a certain amount of time, e.g. 5 minutes. You can then try to beat your time or score.

5) As you get closer to the test day, work on getting a balance between speed and accuracy — that's what you're aiming for when you sit the real test.

There are Many Ways to Practise the Skills you Need

The best way to tackle Verbal Reasoning is to do lots of revision and practice. This isn't the only thing that will help though — there are other ways you can hone the skills you need for the test:

1) Read a mix of fiction and non-fiction — poetry, newspapers, novels etc.
2) If you come across any unfamiliar words, look them up in a dictionary. Keeping a vocabulary list is a great way to remember new words.
3) Play word games or do crosswords to build up your vocabulary.
4) Practise your times tables with a friend by taking it in turns to test each other.
5) Play games like 'Twenty Questions' or 'Cluedo' to help you think logically and draw conclusions based on information that you're given.

Alphabet Positions

These pages will make questions on the alphabet as easy as A, B, C...

11+ Example Question

Here's an example of the type of question you might get in the test:

 **If the alphabet was written backwards, which letter would be at position 7?**

> A letter's alphabet position is just the place that it appears in the alphabet if you count from A to Z. For example, the letter 'a' is the first letter of the alphabet, so it has an alphabet position of 1.

- In these questions, you'll need to count forwards or backwards along the alphabet to find the right letter.
- In this example, the answer is 't' because it is the seventh letter in the alphabet if you count back from 'z'.

These questions involve Counting Letters

 **What is the alphabet position of the middle letter of the word POMEGRANATE?**

Method — Find the middle of the word

1) Some trickier questions might not tell you which letter you have to find the alphabet position of — you have to work it out from the information in the question.

2) First you have to find the middle letter of the word. Count how many letters are in the word, add one then halve the number.

    There are 11 letters in 'pomegranate', so 11 + 1 = 12, 12 ÷ 2 = 6. So the middle letter in 'pomegranate' is the sixth letter.

3) Then, count this many letters into the word.

The sixth letter in 'pomegranate' is 'r'.

> Check you've found the middle letter — there should be an equal number of letters either side of it.

4) Count along the alphabet to find the number position of the letter 'r' — the answer is 18.

It's important to read the question carefully...

In Alphabet Positions questions, you may be asked to count forwards or backwards along the alphabet, so make sure you read the instructions in the question carefully before you start counting.

Alphabet Positions

Some questions may ask you to **Remove Letters**

 **EXAMPLE:** **If all the letters in the word WOODCHUCK were removed from the alphabet, which letter would be at position 6 of the new alphabet?**

Method — Cross out the letters

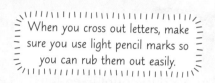
When you cross out letters, make sure you use light pencil marks so you can rub them out easily.

1) You might be given the alphabet in the test, or you may have to write it out yourself.

2) Cross out all the letters in the word 'woodchuck' from the alphabet.

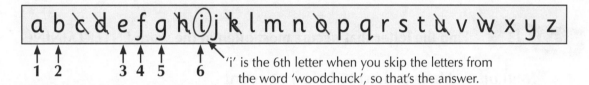

3) Then start at the beginning of the alphabet and count forward 6 letters, skipping the letters that you have crossed out.

a b c d e f g h (i) j k l m n o p q r s t u v w x y z
↑ ↑   ↑ ↑ ↑   ↑
1 2   3 4 5   6

'i' is the 6th letter when you skip the letters from the word 'woodchuck', so that's the answer.

Practice Questions

1) Which letter is at the following position in the alphabet:
   a) 8   b) 12   c) 16   d) 22?

2) If the alphabet was written backwards, which letter would be at position:

   a) 9   b) 14   c) 20   d) 24?

3) What is the alphabet position of the middle letter of the word:
   a) PLUNDER   b) OCTOPUS   c) RASPBERRY?

4) If all the letters in the word **CANDYFLOSS** were removed from the alphabet, which letter would be at position **12** of the new alphabet?

5) If all the letters in the word **MITTENS** were removed from the alphabet, which letter would be at position **20** of the new alphabet?

Use a copy of the alphabet to help you...
TEST TIP If you're not given the alphabet in the test, then write it out on a spare piece of paper. You'll probably use it several times, so count the letters to make sure there are 26.

Identify a Letter From a Clue

Don't be left in the dark — read these pages to become an alphabet ace...

11+ Example Question

Here is an <u>example</u> of the sort of question you might get in the <u>test</u>:

> **EXAMPLE:** **Find the letter that occurs most often in the word OBNOXIOUS.**

- You need to <u>count</u> each letter that occurs in the word you're given. The letter that appears <u>most</u> is the answer.
- The answer to the question above is '<u>o</u>' because it occurs three times in 'obnoxious', which is <u>more</u> than any of the other letters.

Go through the **Letters** in the word **Carefully**

> **EXAMPLE:** **Find the letter that occurs most often in the word ENTERTAINING.**

Method — Make a chart to help you count

1) Even if you think you can see the answer <u>straight away</u>, use this method to <u>check</u> that you've <u>chosen the right letter</u>.

2) Go through the word and count <u>how many times</u> each <u>letter</u> appears.

'e' appears twice. →

> It might help to cross off each letter as you count it so you don't accidentally count the same letter twice.

3) Keep <u>count</u> on a piece of paper — drawing a <u>table</u> like the one below is a <u>good idea</u>. The letter with the <u>highest number</u> will be the answer.

'n' is the answer because it occurs more times than any of the other letters.

> Make sure you read the question carefully — it won't always ask you to find the letter that appears most often.

Every minute counts in the test...

TEST TIP — Don't waste time thinking about the meaning of the word in the question — you only have to count how many times a letter appears, not understand what the word means.

Identify a Letter From a Clue

You might have to look at **Several Different Words**

**EXAMPLE:** Find the letter that appears twice in HOBBYHORSE, twice in HOTHOUSE and once in CHOCOLATE.

Method — Count each letter

1) Take the <u>first word</u>. Find the letters that appear <u>twice</u>.

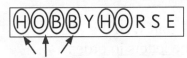

'h', 'o' and 'b' all appear twice — any of these letters could be the answer.

It might help to cross out any letters that definitely aren't right.

2) Look at the <u>second word</u>. <u>Count</u> how many times 'h', 'o' and 'b' appear — you can <u>ignore</u> all the <u>other letters</u> because they <u>don't appear twice</u> in the first word.

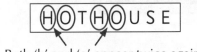

Both 'h' and 'o' appear twice again.

Remember that you're looking for the same letter across all three words.

3) Look at the <u>third word</u>. This time, look for the letter that <u>only</u> appears <u>once</u> in this word, but <u>twice</u> in the <u>other two words</u>. <u>Count</u> how many times 'h' and 'o' appear.

'h' appears once and 'o' appears twice — 'h' is the answer.

Practice Questions

1) Find the letter that occurs most often in the word:
   a) **NOTORIOUS**   b) **FEBRUARY**   c) **SHIPMENTS**

2) Find the letter that occurs twice in the word:
   a) **SHALLOW**   b) **RESPLENDENT**   c) **HANDCUFFS**

3) Find the letter that occurs twice in **DEADEN**, once in **DANCER** and once in **DANDELION**.

Don't rush when you're counting letters...

If you have to find a letter that occurs in several different words, make sure you go through each word carefully so you know how often the letter appears in each one before you start answering.

Alphabetical Order

You need to know your alphabet upside down and inside out for these questions...

11+ Example Question

Here's a sample Alphabetical Order question:

If you arrange the following words in alphabetical order, which comes fourth?

Repays, Racoon, Repeal, Ripped, Repair

- Put the words in alphabetical order — if the words start with the same first letter, you'll need to look at the rest of the letters in order.
- The answer is 'repeal' — the order is racoon, repair, repays, repeal, ripped.

Look at the Start of each word for Forwards questions

EXAMPLE: **If you arrange the following words in alphabetical order, which comes third?**

Duller, Dancer, Dangle, Danger, Dinner

Method — Look at each letter in turn

1) Look at the first letter of each word to see if this will help you put the words in order.

Duller, Dancer, Dangle, Danger, Dinner ← They all begin with 'd', so this doesn't help you.

2) Look at the next letter. Go through the words letter by letter until you find the answer.

Duller, Dancer, Dangle, Danger, Dinner → Three words have the second letter 'a', so the answer will be 'dancer', 'dangle' or 'danger'. They all have the same third letter too, 'n', so you'll have to look at the fourth letter.
5th   4th

Dancer, Dangle, Danger → The fourth letter of 'dancer' is 'c', so it comes first alphabetically. The other two words have the same fourth letter — 'g', so you'll have to look at the fifth letter.
1st

Dangle, Danger → 'e' comes before 'l' so 'danger' is second alphabetically. 'Dangle' is third — which makes it the answer.
3rd   2nd

Alphabetical Order

Look at the last letter first for **Backwards** questions

 **EXAMPLE:** **If you spell the following words backwards, then put them in alphabetical order, which comes second?**

Rapidly, Cleverly, Spooky, Happily, Unkindly

Method — Look at the end of the word

1) Look at the <u>last letter</u> of each word to start putting the words in <u>alphabetical order</u>.

Rapidly, Cleverly, Spooky, Happily, Unkindly ← All the words end with 'y', so you'll need to look at more of the letters.

2) Take the <u>next letter back</u> from the <u>end</u> of each word and <u>work backwards</u> until you can <u>answer</u> the question.

'Spooky' has 'k' as the second letter back, and 'k' comes before 'l'. So 'spooky' would come first alphabetically. → Rapid**l**y, Cleve**rl**y, Spooky, Happi**l**y, Unkind**l**y
1st

Rapi**d**ly, Cleverly, Happily, Unkin**d**ly ← 'Rapidly' and 'unkindly' both have 'd' as the third letter back, and 'd' comes before 'i' and 'r' in the alphabet. So one of these words will be the answer.
5th   4th

'Rapidly' has 'i' as the fourth letter back, whereas 'unkindly' has 'n' as the fourth letter back. 'Rapidly' would be second written backwards — so that's the answer. → Rap**i**dly, Unki**n**dly
2nd   3rd

Practice Questions

1) If you arrange the following words in alphabetical order, which comes fourth?

Confuse, Confides, Confront, Confine, Conference

2) If you spell the following words backwards, then put them in alphabetical order, which comes third?

Irate, Complicate, Deliberate, Frustrate, Inmate

 ## Write out the words if you're stuck...

If you find it tricky to visualise the order of letters in backwards questions when you're revising, it might help if you write out the words backwards on a spare piece of paper.

Practice Questions

You're nearly finished with the Alphabet Section — all that's left to do now is to answer these practice questions. They'll help you to practise working with the alphabet in different ways.

Alphabet Positions

> Answer the questions below. Use the alphabet to help you.
>
> A B C D E F G H I J K L M N O P Q R S T U V W X Y Z
>
> Look at this example:
>
> **Example:** Which letter is at position 3 in the alphabet? ___C___

1. Which letter is at the following position in the alphabet?
   a) 7   b) 10   c) 19   d) 24

2. If the alphabet was written backwards, which letter would be at position:
   a) 6   b) 12   c) 17   d) 22

3. What is the alphabet position of the first letter of the word:
   a) DAWDLE   b) RACKET   c) LOLLIPOP   d) PIGEON

4. What is the alphabet position of the middle letter of the word:
   a) AWFUL   b) FLOWERS   c) CACKLED   d) COCONUT

5. If all the letters in the word **BIRTHDAY** were removed from the alphabet, which letter would be at position **6** in the new alphabet? _____

6. If all the letters in the word **HERITAGE** were removed from the alphabet, which letter would be at position **16** in the new alphabet? _____

7. If all the letters in the word **ARTISTIC** were removed from the alphabet, what alphabet position would the letter **N** occupy? _____

8. If all the vowels in the word **AQUARIUM** were removed from the alphabet, what alphabet position would the letter **V** occupy? _____

9. If all the consonants in the word **CHIPMUNK** were removed from the alphabet, what alphabet position would the letter **R** occupy? _____

Practice Questions

Identify a Letter from a Clue

Find the letter that the clue refers to. Make sure your answer is correct for all parts of the clue. Look at this example:

Example: Find the letter that occurs most often in **CURRICULUM**. __U__

Find the letter that occurs:

10. once in **STRATEGY** and twice in **REABSORB**. _____

11. most often in **ANCIENT**, **ANTENNA** and **ANNOYING**. _____

12. once in **GALACTIC**, once in **GRIDLOCK**,
    but not in **GRASPING**. _____

13. once in **SUPERPOWERS**, once in **RENOUNCED**
    and twice in **ACCOMMODATE**. _____

Alphabetical Order

Answer the questions below. Use the alphabet to help you.

A B C D E F G H I J K L M N O P Q R S T U V W X Y Z

14. If you arrange the following words in alphabetical order, which comes fourth?

    a) Medieval, Melody, Merriment, Meadows _____

    b) Prepped, Precipice, Prevail, Prefaced _____

    c) Tantrum, Tantalise, Tangled, Tangible _____

15. If you spell the following words backwards, then put
    them in alphabetical order, which word comes second?

    a) Entertaining, Prizewinning, Everlasting, Sightseeing _____

    b) Authenticity, Invincibility, Tranquillity, Eccentricity _____

    c) Unintended, Absentminded, Barricaded, Rescinded _____

Preparing for the Test

Make sure you know how words are made — it'll help you to do well with these questions.

Lots of words follow **Spelling Rules**

Whether you're <u>solving an anagram</u> or looking for <u>hidden words</u>, it'll
help if you can <u>recognise common spelling patterns</u> that occur in words.

Patterns at the **Start** of words

1) Words can <u>start</u> with <u>any letter</u> of the alphabet, but not <u>any combination of letters</u>.

2) You'll see 'b', 'c', 'f', 'g', 'p' or 't' <u>before</u> 'l' or 'r', but <u>never after</u> 'l' or 'r' at the <u>start of a word</u>.

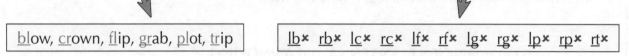

<u>b</u>low, <u>c</u>rown, <u>f</u>lip, <u>gr</u>ab, <u>p</u>lot, <u>tr</u>ip   <u>lb</u>✗   <u>rb</u>✗   <u>lc</u>✗   <u>rc</u>✗   <u>lf</u>✗   <u>rf</u>✗   <u>lg</u>✗   <u>rg</u>✗   <u>lp</u>✗   <u>rp</u>✗   <u>rt</u>✗

3) '<u>h</u>' is common after '<u>c</u>', '<u>s</u>', '<u>t</u>' and '<u>w</u>'. ⟶   <u>c</u>hip, <u>s</u>hop, <u>th</u>is, <u>wh</u>en

4) A <u>prefix</u> can be added to the <u>start</u> of a word to <u>change</u> its <u>meaning</u>, for example:

in- (inedible, indescribable)   dis- (disappear, dislike)

un- (unlock, untidy)

Patterns in the **Middle** of words

1) Almost all words contain <u>vowels</u>. Some patterns of vowels appear <u>frequently</u>, for example:

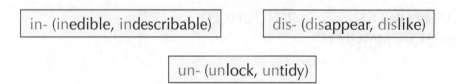

ee   oo   ou   ie   ea   seen   look   pout   diet   tear

2) Some vowels <u>rarely</u> appear together, for example, '<u>uo</u>', '<u>iu</u>', '<u>ae</u>'.

3) <u>Double consonants</u> in the <u>middle of words</u> are common — you'll often come across '<u>tt</u>',
'<u>ss</u>' or '<u>pp</u>', but it's less likely you'll see a word with '<u>hh</u>', '<u>vv</u>', '<u>jj</u>', '<u>ww</u>' or '<u>xx</u>'.

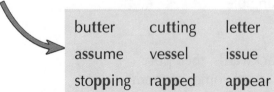

butter	cutting	letter
assume	vessel	issue
stopping	rapped	appear

4) If you can recognise common <u>vowel</u> and <u>consonant</u> patterns that appear in the middle
of words, such as '<u>per</u>', '<u>our</u>', '<u>are</u>' and '<u>ate</u>', it'll help to improve your <u>spelling</u>.

Preparing for the Test

Patterns at the **End** of words

1) Some <u>combinations</u> of <u>consonants</u> are often found at the <u>end</u> of words. For <u>example</u>:

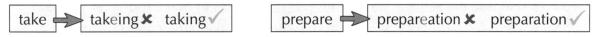

church   clock   fifth   cash   harm   high   string

2) <u>Suffixes</u> come at the <u>end</u> of words — they can be <u>verb</u> endings like '<u>-ed</u>', <u>plurals</u> such as '<u>-s</u>' or <u>adverb</u> endings like '<u>-ly</u>'. Here are some <u>common suffixes</u>:

-ition (addition)   -ity (humidity)   -ful (careful)   -ing (playing)   -y (sandy)

3) Remember, when you <u>add a suffix</u> the <u>spelling</u> of the root word can <u>change</u>:

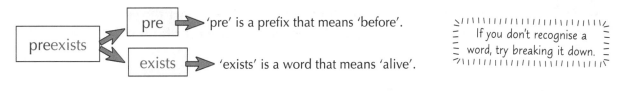

take ➡ takeing ✘ taking ✓   prepare ➡ prepareation ✘ preparation ✓

Use **Spelling Patterns** to help you answer questions

1) If you know a bit about <u>prefixes</u> it can help you work out the <u>meaning</u> of words, for example:

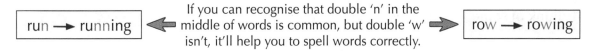

preexists → pre → 'pre' is a prefix that means 'before'.

exists → 'exists' is a word that means 'alive'.

If you don't recognise a word, try breaking it down.

2) Learn some common <u>patterns</u> in the <u>middle</u> of words — it'll help with your <u>spelling</u>.

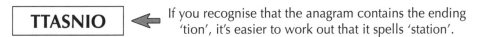

run → running   If you can recognise that double 'n' in the middle of words is common, but double 'w' isn't, it'll help you to spell words correctly.   row → rowing

3) Think about <u>word endings</u> to help you to solve anagrams.

TTASNIO   If you recognise that the anagram contains the ending 'tion', it's easier to work out that it spells 'station'.

Practice Questions

1) Can you think of any words that start with the following letters?
   a) str   b) blr   c) shr   d) ds

2) Unscramble the following anagrams:
   a) YZCAR   b) IGNMXI   c) NTALEMECP

Don't let tricky spellings catch you out...

REVISION TIP

If you keep spelling a word incorrectly while you're revising, write it on a sticky note and put it somewhere you'll see every day. This will help the right spelling stick in your mind.

Section Two — Making Words

Missing Letters

Some letters have gone missing. Looks like another excuse for a Verbal Reasoning question.

11+ Example Question

Here's a sample 11+ style question:

Find the letter that will finish the first word and start the second word of each pair. The same letter must be used for both pairs.

dar (__) arn   tal (__) ast

- You need to add the same letter to both sets of brackets to make four new words.
- The answer is '<u>e</u>' — it works with all four words to make <u>dare</u>, <u>earn</u>, <u>tale</u> and <u>east</u>.

Think of some Words that could be made

Find the letter that will finish the first word and start the second word of each pair. The same letter must be used for both pairs.

gri (__) ain   sea (__) ale

Method 1 — Brainstorming

1) <u>Read</u> the question. Look at the <u>first set</u> of words and think of some <u>four-letter</u> words that start with 'gri_'.

     gri (__) ain → grid   grim   grin   grip   grit

     'd', 'm', 'n', 'p' and 't' can all be added to 'gri_' to make a new word.

2) Add 'd', 'm', 'n', 'p' and 't' to the start of _ain to try and make a new word. →

     dain ✗   main ✓   nain ✗
     pain ✓   tain ✗

3) So '<u>m</u>' and '<u>p</u>' work for the first set — they make the words '<u>gri(m)ain</u>' and '<u>gri(p)ain</u>'.

4) Only <u>one letter</u> will work for <u>both sets</u>, so you need to try <u>both letters</u> in the <u>second set</u>.

     sea (<u>m</u>) ale ← 'm' makes the words ✓ 'seam' and 'male'.

     sea (<u>p</u>) ale ← 'p' makes the word 'pale' ✗ but 'seap' isn't a word.

5) '<u>m</u>' works with <u>all four</u> words, so that's the <u>answer</u>.

Missing Letters

Try each letter in the **Alphabet**

 **KEY EXAMPLE:**

loo (__) ite   lea (__) ill

Method 2 — Going through the alphabet

1) If you <u>can't think</u> of a letter that works for all the words, and you don't have the multiple-choice options to help you narrow the answer down, try <u>each letter</u> of the <u>alphabet</u> in turn.

2) If you have a spare piece of paper, it may help to <u>write</u> the <u>alphabet lengthways</u> down the side.

3) Take the <u>first word</u>, run the alphabet strip <u>alongside</u> the word with the <u>missing letter</u> and <u>jot</u> down any combinations that work.

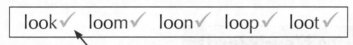

The letters 'k', 'm', 'n', 'p' and 't' can be added to the end of 'loo_' to make a new word.

4) Once you have a list of letters that complete 'loo_', try them with '_ite'.

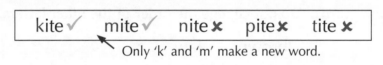

Only 'k' and 'm' make a new word.

> Watch out for words that sound like real words, but are spelled incorrectly, like 'tite'.

5) Try the remaining letters in the <u>second pair</u> of words.

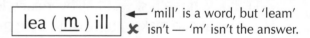

lea (__k__) ill ← 'leak' and 'kill' ✓ are both words.

lea (__m__) ill ← 'mill' is a word, but 'leam' ✗ isn't — 'm' isn't the answer.

6) 'k' works with <u>all four</u> words, so that's the <u>answer</u>.

Practice Questions

1) Find the letter that will finish the first word and start the second word.

   a) cal (__) lap   b) to (__) ou   c) to (__) lf   d) sli (__) ix

2) Find the letter that will finish the first word and start the second word of each pair. The same letter must be used for both pairs.

   a) do (__) ap   plu (__) ram   b) wa (__) oon   mis (__) un

 TEST TIP

These questions are a bit easier in a multiple-choice test...

If you're doing a multiple-choice test, you'll be given five options, and the answer can only be one of the letters you've been given. Try out each option to see which one works.

Move a Letter

Move a Letter questions test how well you can recognise words. Read on for some handy methods.

Here's an example of an 11+ style question you might find in the test:

> **KEY EXAMPLE:** **Remove one letter from the first word and add it to the second word to make two new words. Do not change the order of the other letters.**
>
> trust   say

- You need to remove a letter from 'trust' to make a new word and add the same letter to 'say' to make a new word.
- The answer is 't' — the two new words are rust and stay.

These questions involve making **New Words**

> **KEY EXAMPLE:** **Remove one letter from the first word and add it to the second word to make two new words. Do not change the order of the other letters.**
>
> brown   law

Method 1 — Cover each letter

1) Look at the first word. Cover each letter in turn to see if you can make a new word by removing a letter.

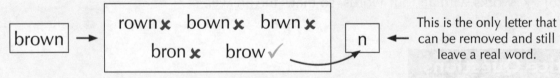

brown → rown ✘ bown ✘ brwn ✘ bron ✘ brow ✓ → n

This is the only letter that can be removed and still leave a real word.

2) Try adding the letter 'n' to the word 'law' to make a new word.

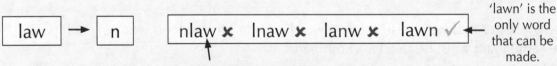

law → n nlaw ✘ lnaw ✘ lanw ✘ lawn ✓

'lawn' is the only word that can be made.

The letter could be added to the **beginning**, **middle** or **end** of the second word, so you need to try the letter in all the different positions.

3) So 'n' is the letter that moves, and the new words are 'brow' and 'lawn'.

Move a Letter

Sometimes you might get a **Trickier Question**

 **Remove one letter from the first word and add it to the second word to make two new words. Do not change the order of the other letters.**

plain   cap

Method 2 — Trial and error

1) Sometimes, you might be able to make <u>more than one</u> word by <u>removing different letters</u> from the first word.

2) Look at the <u>first word</u>. <u>Cover</u> each letter in turn to see if you can make a <u>new word</u> by <u>removing a letter</u>.

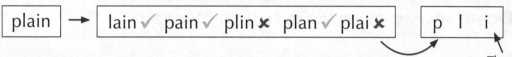

| plain | → | lain ✓ pain ✓ plin ✗ plan ✓ plai ✗ | | p l i |

These are the letters that can be removed and still leave a real word.

3) Try each of these letters with 'cap' to see if it makes a <u>new word</u>. <u>Only one</u> of the letters should work.

cap	→	p		pcap ✗ cpap ✗ capp ✗ capp ✗
cap	→	l		lcap ✗ clap ✓ calp ✗ capl ✗
cap	→	i		icap ✗ ciap ✗ caip ✗ capi ✗

4) So 'l' is the letter that moves, and the new words are 'pain' and 'clap'.

Practice Questions

Remove one letter from the first word and add it to the second word to make two new words. Do not change the order of the other letters.

1) clone   gad
2) split   eel
3) pride   air

4) crook   cow
5) clean   cap
6) wheat   sell

Use your vocabulary knowledge to check your answer...

If you're unsure whether you've made a correctly spelled new word, try comparing it to words that you already know. In the example above, 'clap' looks similar to words such as 'slap' and 'flap'.

Hidden Word

Get yourself ready for some Hidden Word questions — find the words to earn the marks.

11+ Example Question

This is an example of the sort of <u>Hidden Word</u> question you can expect to find in the <u>test</u>:

> **KEY EXAMPLE:** **In the sentence below a four-letter word is hidden at the end of one word and the start of the next. Find the pair of words which contains the hidden word.**
>
> Rashida built a rocket in her back garden.

- Spot a <u>pair of words</u> that have a word hidden at the <u>end</u> of one word and the <u>start</u> of the next.
- The answer is '<u>her back</u>' — the hidden word is '<u>herb</u>', which is formed from '<u>her</u>' and '<u>b</u>ack'.

Narrow Down your search by Focussing on Vowels

> **KEY EXAMPLE:** **In the sentence below a four-letter word is hidden at the end of one word and the start of the next. Find the pair of words which contains the hidden word.**
>
> Don't forget to clean each one twice.

Method 1 — Look at the vowels

1) <u>Read</u> the sentence and <u>identify</u> all the words that <u>begin</u> or <u>end</u> with <u>vowels</u>.

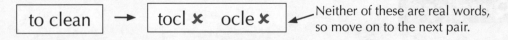

Don't forget to clean each one twice. ← It's almost certain that the hidden word will have a vowel in it, so looking at the words that start or end with vowels can help you find it quickly.

2) If the word <u>ends</u> with a <u>vowel</u>, take the word to its <u>right</u> and look for the <u>hidden word</u>.

to clean → tocl ✗   ocle ✗ ← Neither of these are real words, so move on to the next pair.

3) If the word <u>starts</u> with a <u>vowel</u>, take the word to its <u>left</u> and look for the <u>hidden word</u>.

clean each → eane ✗   anea ✗   neac ✗ ← None of these are real words, so move on to the next pair.

4) If the word <u>starts</u> and <u>ends</u> with a <u>vowel</u>, take the word to its <u>left</u> and <u>right</u> and look for the <u>hidden word</u>.

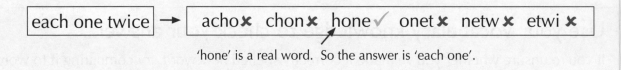

each one twice → acho ✗   chon ✗   hone ✓   onet ✗   netw ✗   etwi ✗

'hone' is a real word. So the answer is 'each one'.

Hidden Word

Check each **Pair Of Words**

**KEY EXAMPLE:** In the sentence below a four-letter word is hidden at the end of one word and the start of the next. Find the pair of words which contains the hidden word.

Dave hates lumpy powdered custard.

Method 2 — Rule out options one by one

1) If looking at the vowels <u>doesn't work</u>, look at each pair of words in turn — start with the <u>first two words</u>.

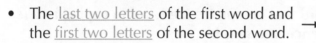

2) Look at:

- The <u>last three letters</u> of the first word, and the <u>first letter</u> of the second word. → aveh ✗

- The <u>last two letters</u> of the first word and the <u>first two letters</u> of the second word. → veha ✗

- The <u>last letter</u> of the first word, and the <u>first three letters</u> of the second word. → ehat ✗

> You won't have time to write out all the combinations in the test, so use two pencils to cover up the letters either side of the four letters you're looking at.

ve ha

None of these combinations make a word.

3) If the first pair of words <u>doesn't work</u>, move on to the <u>second</u> and <u>third</u> words in the sentence and <u>repeat</u> the process.

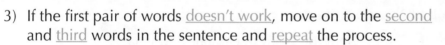

hates lumpy → tesl ✗   eslu ✗   slum ✓ ← 'slum' is a word.

4) There should only be <u>one correct answer</u>, so the hidden word is '<u>slum</u>' and the answer is '<u>hates lumpy</u>'.

Practice Questions

In each sentence below a four-letter word is hidden at the end of one word and the start of the next. Find the hidden four-letter word.

1) The turnip eaten yesterday was unripe.

2) Rebecca keeps slugs in her room.

3) Mr Gregory also farms wheat.

4) I like my placid old dog.

5) His banjo keeps me up at night.

6) My burger is covered in cheese.

If you're stuck, make a sensible guess...

TEST TIP If you look at all the possible combinations and still can't find the hidden word, pick the option that seems the most sensible to you. Even if you don't recognise the word 'slum', it looks a lot more plausible than letter combinations like 'aveh' or 'eslu'.

Find the Missing Word

You'll need a good vocab and an understanding of how words are made to answer these questions.

11+ Example Question

Take a look at the question <u>below</u> — it's the sort of thing you can expect in the <u>test</u>.

 **Find the three-letter word that completes the word in capital letters, and so finishes the sentence in a sensible way.**

Jaguars and gorillas live in the **RAINEST**.

- You need to add a <u>three-letter word</u> to **RAINEST** to make a <u>word</u> which finishes the sentence.
- The answer is '<u>FOR</u>' — when you add it to **RAINEST**, you get **RAIN<u>FOR</u>EST**.

Use your knowledge of **Word Types**

 **Find the three-letter word that completes the word in capital letters, and so finishes the sentence in a sensible way.**

There was a **TREDOUS** bang when the washing machine exploded.

Method 1 — Look at the word type

1) Read the sentence. <u>Think</u> about the word in capitals and what sort of word would <u>make sense</u> in the <u>context</u> of the sentence.

> There was a **TREDOUS** bang when the washing machine exploded.

It looks like the missing word is describing the noun 'bang', so it must be an adjective.

It's describing the sound of a washing machine exploding so the adjective might mean 'loud' or 'big'.

2) Look at the word in capitals <u>again</u>. You need to find an <u>adjective</u> that means '<u>loud</u>' or '<u>big</u>', that is <u>ten letters long</u> and that contains the letters **TREDOUS**.

> **TREMENDOUS** ◄— 'Tremendous' is an adjective that means 'big' that is 10 letters long.

3) Check that the word <u>makes sense</u> in the sentence.

> There was a **TREMENDOUS** bang when the washing machine exploded.

4) Check that the missing letters makes a <u>three-letter word</u>.

> **TRE<u>MEN</u>DOUS** —► The missing three letters spell 'men', so that's your answer.

Find the Missing Word

Use **Prefixes** and **Suffixes** to help you work out the answer

 **KEY EXAMPLE:** The complicated film **CONFD** me.

Method 2 — Think about the order of the letters

Have a look at p.12 for a reminder of letters that don't go together.

1) <u>Look</u> at the word in <u>capitals</u>. Try to identify any combinations of letters that <u>don't look right</u>.

The complicated film **CONFD** me.	The complicated film **CONFD** me.

'CON' looks sensible — it's found in words like 'contain', 'contour', 'concern'.

'NFD' looks less recognisable. There are three consonants together. Looks like there's a vowel or two missing...

2) Once you've identified the part of the word that looks <u>strange</u>, think about the <u>word type</u> and whether that gives you any <u>clues</u> to what the <u>missing word</u> could be.

The complicated film **CONFD** me.

It may help you to write the word out with gaps where you think the missing letters go.

There aren't any verbs in the sentence, so the word in capitals must be a **verb**. The word in capitals ends in 'D', so the word could be in the past tense. That would mean that there's an 'e' missing from the 'ed' ending. ⟶ **CONF _ _ E D**

3) Try to think of some <u>eight-letter verbs</u> that start with '<u>conf</u>' and end with '<u>ed</u>'.

confided	confined	confused

'confided' and 'confined' are both words, but the missing letters 'ide' and 'ine' don't spell new words.

'confused' is a real word and the missing letters spell the word 'use'.

4) Put the <u>complete word</u> into the sentence to check that it <u>makes sense</u>.

The complicated film **CONFUSED** me.

✓ 'confused' makes sense in the context of the sentence, so the answer is 'use'.

Practice Questions

Find the three-letter word that completes the word in capital letters, and so finishes the sentence in a sensible way.

1) The teacher **FNED** at the naughty child.
2) We **GLSED** a deer running through the trees.

 REVISION TIP

Revising your letter patterns will help with these questions...

Crosswords are a fun way to improve your ability to identify common letter patterns and figure out missing letters. They're also great for helping you to expand your vocabulary.

Use a Rule to Make a Word

This question type can be one of the trickier ones on the paper — don't worry, we've got it covered.

 **11+ Example** Question

Take a look at the question <u>below</u> — it's the sort of thing you can expect in the <u>test</u>.

> **KEY EXAMPLE:** The words in the second set follow the same pattern as the words in the first set. Find the missing word to complete the second set.
>
> wit (eat) pea   cab (?) ewe

- Find the letters <u>taken</u> from the <u>outer words</u> in the first set to make the <u>word in brackets</u>.
- You need to use the <u>same pattern</u> to work out the answer to the <u>second set of words</u>.
- The answer is '<u>web</u>' — the pattern uses the second and third letters of the right-hand word ('<u>w</u>' and '<u>e</u>'), followed by the last letter of the left-hand word ('<u>b</u>').

These questions test your **Ability** to spot **Patterns**

>  **KEY EXAMPLE:** The words in the second set follow the same pattern as the words in the first set. Find the missing word to complete the second set.
>
> sag (sat) rut   but (?) fog

Method 1 — Spot the pattern

1) Look at the <u>first group</u> of words. Take the <u>word in brackets</u>, and <u>identify</u> the <u>letters</u> that also appear in the <u>two outer words</u>.

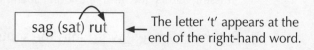

's' and 'a' appear at the start of the left-hand word. → sag (sat) rut   sag (sat) rut ← The letter 't' appears at the end of the right-hand word.

2) <u>Identify the pattern</u> which has been applied to the two outer words to make the <u>word in brackets</u>.

Put the **first two letters** of the **left-hand word** together with the **last letter** of the **right-hand word**.

3) <u>Apply the pattern</u> to the <u>second set</u> of words.

but (bug) fog ← Using the same pattern as the first set of words, the word 'bug' is made.

Make sure you mark the right choice on your answer sheet. There may be some similar words designed to trick you.

4) <u>Check</u> that your answer is a <u>real word</u> and is the <u>same length</u> as the word in the <u>first set of brackets</u>.

5) If you're using a <u>multiple-choice</u> answer sheet, your answer should be <u>one</u> of the <u>five options</u>.

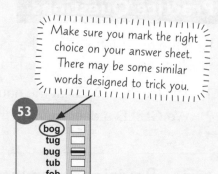

53
bog
tug
bug
tub
fob

Use a Rule to Make a Word

Write down the options for **Each Letter**

 **KEY EXAMPLE:** The words in the second set follow the same pattern as the words in the first set. Find the missing word to complete the second set.

rely (yell) tale   scum (?) mane

Method 2 — Write down what each letter could be

1) If a letter from the word in brackets appears <u>more than once in the outer words</u>, you'll need to use a <u>different method</u> to help you answer the question.

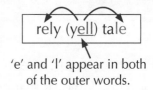

'e' and 'l' appear in both of the outer words.

2) <u>Identify</u> which letter has been <u>taken</u> from the <u>outer words</u> to make the first letter of the <u>word in brackets</u>.

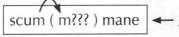 ← 3) Find the <u>equivalent letter</u> in the second set.

4) Move on to the <u>next letter</u>. If a letter appears in <u>both</u> of the outer words, <u>write down</u> both the <u>equivalent letters</u> from the second set.

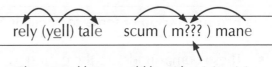

The second letter could be either 'c' or 'e'.

5) <u>Repeat</u> this method until you've written down the <u>possible letters</u> for <u>each</u> letter position of the <u>word</u>.

6) There should only be <u>one combination</u> of letters that makes a <u>new word</u> — so the answer for this question is '<u>menu</u>'.

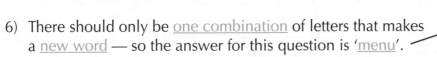

Practice Questions

The words in the second set follow the same pattern as the words in the first set. Find the missing word to complete the second set.

1) tap (pod) nod   son (?) rib

2) deal (ode) crop   spin (?) load

3) poet (port) part   wept (?) stag

4) flow (glow) logs   earl (?) ripe

 ## Rule out as many of the options as you can...

TEST TIP In a multiple-choice test, you can use the options to help you. If you can work out a few letters, it might be enough to give you the answer, or at least rule out a couple of options.

Compound Words

Compound words are made up of two separate words joined together — like 'milkshake'.

11+ Example Question

This is what a Compound Words question might look like:

 **KEY EXAMPLE:** Underline a word from the first set, followed by a word from the second set, that go together to form a new word.

(up down side) (back front forward)

- Pick two words, one from each set of brackets, that make a new word when they're combined.
- Don't pick words that go together, e.g. 'fish' and 'chips', or hyphenated words such as 'full-time'.
- The correct pair, 'up' and 'front', can be combined to make the new word 'upfront'.

There are different types of Compound Words

The Pronunciation of some compounds Won't Change

- These compounds are the easiest to spot, and should be the types of compounds you come across most often in the test.
- Here are some examples:

The pronunciation for both parts of the compound stays the same.

| blackbird | update | below | antelope |

The Pronunciation of some compounds will Change

- These compounds are trickier to spot because the pronunciation of one, or both, parts of the compound change.
- Here are some examples:

feat + her = feather   arm + our = armour

way + ward = wayward   agree + able = agreeable

 REVISION TIP

Don't get caught out by changing pronunciation...

Think about whether any of the words in the brackets can be pronounced another way. This might help you to spot trickier compound words where the pronunciation changes.

Section Two — Making Words

Compound Words

 **Underline a word from the first set, followed by a word from the second set, that go together to form a new word.**

(park sleep mass) (per age king)

Method — Rule out the options that don't work

1) Take the first word from the first set of brackets and try combining it with each word in the second set of brackets to see whether it makes a new word.

parkper ✘	parkage ✘	parkking ✘

'parkking' sounds as if it could be right, but it's not spelled correctly.

2) If the first word doesn't make a new word, take the second word in the first bracket and repeat the process.

sleepper ✘	sleepage ✘	sleepking ✘

For a bit more on common double letters, turn back to p.12.

'sleepper' sounds OK when you say it aloud, but when you write the word as a compound, it isn't spelt correctly.

3) Try the last word in the first bracket and repeat the process.

massper ✘	massage ✓	massking ✘

'massking' sounds as if it could be right, but it's got an 's' too many.

Separately, 'mass' and 'age' don't sound like they make a new word, but when you write them down they make a word — 'massage'.

4) So the correct answer is 'massage'.

Practice Questions

Choose a word from the first set, followed by a word from the second set, that go together to form a new word.

1) (pat rib rot) (tin ten bin)   3) (drag pull push) (in on an)

2) (am be is) (wear ware were)   4) (clot clog clump) (her he she)

Some Compound Words questions might be a little different...

Another type of Compound Words question will ask you to find a word that can go before or after a set of words. You might have to think of a word that can go after 'net', 'foot' and 'meat' to make three new words. The answer to this question would be 'ball' — netball, football and meatball.

Complete a Word Pair

These questions are easier than they look — especially when you have a foolproof method.

11+ Example Question

Here's an example of a <u>Complete a Word Pair</u> question:

Find the word that completes the third pair of words so that it follows the same pattern as the first two pairs.

marks arm   ready ear   glove (?)

- All three pairs of words are formed using the <u>same pattern</u> — you need to work out what the pattern is, and <u>apply</u> it to the third pair to <u>work out the answer</u>.
- The answer is '<u>log</u>' — <u>remove</u> the <u>last two letters</u>, then move the <u>first letter</u> to the <u>end</u> of the word.

There are different types of Pattern

1) You might be asked to <u>remove</u> and <u>rearrange</u> letters, e.g.:

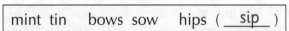

mint tin   bows sow   hips (__sip__) ⬅ The first letter of each pair has been removed and then the last letter has been moved to the front.

2) You might have to <u>spot</u> words that have been written <u>backwards</u>, e.g.:

emit time   keep peek   rats (__star__)

3) You might have to <u>change</u> a letter, e.g.:

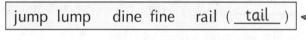

jump lump   dine fine   rail (__tail__) ⬅ The first letter of each word moves along the alphabet two letters each time.

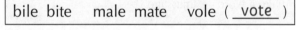

bile bite   male mate   vole (__vote__) ⬅ The 'l' changes to a 't' in each pair.

Use the Most Helpful Pair of Words

extent ten   places ape   inform (?)

Method 1 — Spot the pattern

1) Look at the <u>first pair</u>. Check if any of the letters in the <u>second word</u> are <u>repeated</u> in the <u>first word</u>. In the first pair, the letters '<u>t</u>' and '<u>e</u>' are each used <u>twice</u>.

2) If there are <u>repeated</u> letters, <u>don't waste time</u> trying to solve the first pair — move on to the <u>next pair</u> to see if the pattern is more <u>obvious</u>.

places   ape ⬅ There are no repeated letters — each of the letters in the second word only appears once in the first word.

3) To find the <u>answer</u> you need to take the <u>first</u>, <u>third</u> and <u>fifth</u> letters of 'inform' and arrange them in the order 3rd, 1st, 5th. So the answer is '<u>fir</u>'.

Section Two — Making Words

Complete a Word Pair

Look for the **Easiest Letters** to **Solve**

 **KEY EXAMPLE:**   cabbages sage   wandered dare   focussed (?)

Method 2 — Solve the letters that aren't repeated first

1) Harder questions may have repeated letters in both words.

2) Look at both pairs — the first pair has fewer repeated letters, so use that. Discount any letters that don't appear in the second word.

> cabbages   sage

3) Discount the same letters in the third word.

> focussed ← The first, third and fourth letters of 'cabbages' don't appear in 'sage', so you can discount these letters in 'focussed'.

4) Rearrange the letters in the same pattern as the first pair of words. Leave a gap if you're unsure of a letter. → d __ se

5) If you get most of the word you'll often be able to guess the missing letter. Here, the only letter that fills → dose the gap to make a word is 'o', so the answer is 'dose'.

Practice Questions

Find the word that completes the third pair of words so that it follows the same pattern as the first two pairs.

1) writer rite   shandy hand   tables (?)

2) mobile lob   barber ear   ration (?)

3) fabric cab   jetsam met   caters (?)

4) mammoth ham   million nil   matador (?)

Don't rush when you're working out the answer...

It can be easy to miscount letters, especially if you're rushing. Make sure you count carefully.

Anagram in a Sentence

Anagrams are when the letters in a word are all mixed up, so NAAAMRG is an anagram of anagram.

11+ Example Question

Here's an example of an <u>Anagram in a Sentence</u> question:

EXAMPLE: **Rearrange the letters in capitals to spell a word that completes the sentence in a sensible way.**

The sky turned deep **GANORE** as the sun set.

- You need to <u>unjumble</u> the letters to form a word that <u>makes sense</u>.
- The answer is '<u>ORANGE</u>'. The completed sentence is:
  'The sky turned deep orange as the sun set.'

Try **Writing Out** the letters

EXAMPLE: **Rearrange the letters in capitals to spell a word that completes the sentence in a sensible way.**

The **YGEDER** chicken ate all the corn.

Method 1 — Write the letters out in a circle

1) Read the sentence and look at the <u>anagram</u>.

The **YGEDER** chicken ate all the corn.

If you're struggling to see the word, keep rearranging the letters.

2) If you don't recognise the word straight away, try <u>writing</u> the letters out in a <u>circle</u> to help you spot the word.

You may spot that 'g' and 'r' are often found at the start of words, 'ee' often occurs in the middle, and 'y' is most likely to be found at the end of words.

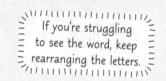

3) Once you think you've found the answer, try it in the sentence to <u>check</u> that it <u>makes sense</u>.

The **GREEDY** chicken ate all the corn. ✓ → So the answer is 'greedy'.

Anagram in a Sentence

Try to spot common **Letter Patterns**

**EXAMPLE:**   I was **NHISUTOG** when I lost my voice.

Method 2 — Think about the word type

1) Read the sentence. Think about what word type the anagram could belong to.

I was (NHISUTOG) when I lost my voice. ← The anagram comes after 'was', so it's likely to be a **verb**. Verbs that follow 'was' often end in 'ed' or 'ing'.

I was (NHISUTOG) when I lost my voice.

The anagram doesn't contain the letters 'ed' but it does contain the letters 'ing', so we can try rearranging the anagram with 'ing' at the end. → **HSUTOING**

2) Look at the rest of the sentence to try and find a clue about the meaning of the anagram.

I was **NHISUTOG** when I lost my voice. → The sentence is about someone who has lost their voice — you lose your voice when you talk a lot or shout.

3) You've worked out that the word is likely to mean 'making a lot of noise', so look at the remaining letters with 'ing' removed to see if words like 'talk', 'shout' 'yell' etc fit.

HSUTO → **SHOUT** → I was **SHOUTING** when I lost my voice. ✓

Practice Questions

Rearrange the letters in capitals to spell a word that completes the sentence in a sensible way.

1) My aunty has five nieces and **WHSEPNE**.

2) It was quite **LCODUY** and cold when we went to the park.

3) I ordered **NEGSLAA** for dinner when I went to the Italian restaurant.

4) He walked **CFURAEYLL** along the tightrope.

5) We visited a **NGLESHI** beach on holiday.

Knowing your word types will help with Anagram questions...

When you're solving an anagram, use the rest of the sentence to help you work out whether it's a noun, verb, adjective or adverb. Try to spot any prefixes or suffixes that are related to that word type, such as 'tion' or 'ment' for nouns, then unscramble the rest of the letters to make the word.

Word Ladders

Word Ladders — your stairway to success....

An 11+ <u>Word Ladder</u> question may look something like this:

 **Change one letter at a time to make the first word into the final word.
The two answers must be real words.**

COPE (_____) (_____) FORT

Method — Change one letter at a time

1) <u>Identify</u> the letter that <u>appears</u> in <u>both</u> the <u>first</u> and <u>last</u> word, in the <u>same position</u>.

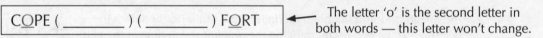

C<u>O</u>PE (_____) (_____) F<u>O</u>RT ← The letter 'o' is the second letter in both words — this letter won't change.

2) <u>Replace</u> the <u>first letter</u> of 'cope' with the first letter of 'fort'. It doesn't make a new word, so replace the <u>third letter</u> of 'cope' with the third letter of 'fort' and so on, until you make a <u>new word</u>.

Remember that you can't switch the letter positions around.

FOPE ✗ FORT   CORE ✓ FORT

3) To find the <u>third word</u>, repeat the same method as before — <u>replace</u> the letters of 'core' with the letters from 'fort' until you make a <u>new word</u>.

FORE ✓ FORT ← Remember, you don't have to change the second or third letters of 'core' because they already match the equivalent letters in 'fort'.

4) With the missing words in place, you should only have to change <u>one letter</u> to <u>make the last word</u>.

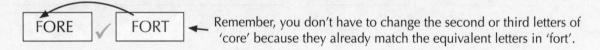

COPE (__CORE__) (__FORE__) FORT ✓

Practice Questions

Change one letter at a time to make the first word into the final word.
The two answers must be real words.

1) SPED (_____) (_____) FLEA   2) CASE (_____) (_____) BOSS

Don't panic if you're not sure about the answer...

All of your answers in a word ladder need to be real words. If you don't recognise any of the possible letter combinations as words that you know, pick the one that sounds most plausible.

Practice Questions

It's time to have a go at some Making Words practice questions to test your skills. If you get stuck on a question, don't worry — have another look at the relevant pages in the section, then try again.

Missing Letters

Find the letter that will finish the first word and start the second word of each pair. The same letter must be used for both pairs. Look at this example:

Example: cas (?) nd   stor (?) mit   ___e___   (**case**, **end**, **store** and **emit**)

1. wis (?) ay   fort (?) one   _____

2. spa (?) ods   mea (?) oun   _____

3. shre (?) isp   ste (?) ay   _____

4. shor (?) ats   ach (?) arn   _____

5. ste (?) ear   stee (?) ace   _____

6. car (?) wes   gap (?) ar   _____

7. hus (?) erb   see (?) ept   _____

8. her (?) ay   wel (?) ire   _____

9. slo (?) ide   ge (?) oil   _____

10. bee (?) ail   the (?) ine   _____

11. ra (?) ave   snu (?) asp   _____

12. hea (?) end   coa (?) eek   _____

Practice Questions

Move a Letter

Remove one letter from the first word and add it to the second word to make two new words. Do not change the order of the other letters. Write the letter that moves on the line. Look at this example.

Example: ahead   got   __a__   (The new words are **head** and **goat**.)

13. ideal   sad   _____

14. bland   pot   _____

15. liked   pin   _____

16. tones   may   _____

17. mouth   men   _____

18. times   for   _____

19. first   ion   _____

20. split   rue   _____

21. bends   had   _____

22. globe   sun   _____

23. drawn   are   _____

24. filed   pan   _____

Practice Questions

Hidden Word

In each sentence below, a four-letter word is hidden at the end of one word and the start of the next. Underline the part of the sentence that contains the hidden word and write the hidden word on the line. Look at this example:

Example: Ta<u>ra ce</u>lebrated her ninth birthday today.   ___race___

25. Pete couldn't buy a green wardrobe anywhere.   _____

26. Having a numb ankle makes walking difficult.   _____

27. Timo gave his turtle another piece of banana.   _____

28. Priya threatened to reveal everybody's secrets.   _____

29. They both used glitter on their paintings.   _____

30. Victor played the banjo in the talent show.   _____

31. The watermelon grew faster in the greenhouse.   _____

32. She wouldn't swap lottery tickets with me.   _____

33. My teacher chooses a star pupil each week.   _____

34. Tamar had to consider entering the dark tunnel.   _____

35. Grandpa gets a fried egg roll for lunch.   _____

36. The dog noticed the bacon lying within reach.   _____

Practice Questions

Find the Missing Word

Find the three-letter word that completes the word in capital letters, and so finishes the sentence in a sensible way. Write your answer on the line. Look at this example:

Example: Alessio hoped that his **WIS** would come true. ___SHE___

37. Yasmin decided to **ARGE** her books in alphabetical order. _____

38. **DESE** his best efforts, Mike couldn't fix his bike. _____

39. Our roof **COLSED** under the weight of the snow. _____

40. Mateo always prepares good arguments for our class **DEES**. _____

41. Pari was **INNANT** about being accused of breaking the vase. _____

42. Ayla is normally very talkative but she was quite **SUBD** today. _____

43. My sister always **FIDS** when she's been sitting still for too long. _____

44. Joe has a lot of **SYMHY** for people when they're upset. _____

45. We had to train our cat to stop **CING** at the sofa. _____

46. Juan **RECED** in disgust when he saw the mouldy bread. _____

47. I went to an art **GERY** and saw a famous painting. _____

48. The elephant watched its step so it didn't **TPLE** on the mouse. _____

Practice Questions

Use a Rule to Make a Word

The words in the second set follow the same pattern as the words in the first set. Find the missing word to complete the second set. Look at this example:

Example: spot (pore) bred   scab (_camp_) imps

49. star (tire) nice   also (_____) lock

50. path (heap) tape   club (_____) bite

51. able (bear) area   liar (_____) beds

52. airy (part) trap   inch (_____) earn

53. sole (sea) easy   cape (_____) apes

54. inert (rent) nasty   seats (_____) snake

55. pips (pier) role   reef (_____) torn

56. cell (lie) tier   neon (_____) onto

57. fried (rife) front   veers (_____) abate

58. fill (toil) note   unto (_____) nets

59. echo (tone) neat   once (_____) rich

60. game (mate) time   sent (_____) skin

Practice Questions

Compound Words

Mark a word from the first set, followed by a word from the second set, that go together to form a new word.

Example: (of tell <u>sea</u>) (way <u>side</u> fair) (the new word is 'seaside')

61. (way up down)   (out here lift)

62. (bill err over)   (grown end bored)

63. (inn near any)   (twine wear more)

64. (off disc space)   (ring over out)

65. (way waste much)   (full word land)

66. (in for home)   (age maid past)

67. (man be shut)   (ate nest have)

68. (prom plus not)   (side point ice)

69. (low life sum)   (thing like fall)

70. (swim more back)   (ring duct over)

71. (add be date)   (fore apt span)

72. (time tale nit)   (wear bone line)

Practice Questions

Complete a Word Pair

> Find the word that completes the third pair of words so that it follows the same pattern as the first two pairs. Look at this example:
>
> **Example:** decodes cod   charter art   patient ___tie___

73. someone son   hundred hue   failure _____

74. operate ore   request rut   habitat _____

75. villain ail   harmony oar   curious _____

76. decent dent   figure fire   losing _____

77. flow wolf   pets step   pots _____

78. breach acre   frozen zero   narrow _____

79. middle idle   robust oust   bounce _____

80. empower were   servant ants   exhibit _____

81. closely sly   battery try   adorned _____

82. event vet   doubt out   draft _____

83. trap part   keep peek   edit _____

84. rant want   hare mare   bear _____

Practice Questions

Anagram in a Sentence

> Rearrange the letters in capitals to spell a word that completes the sentence in a sensible way. Write the new word on the line. Look at this example:
>
> **Example:** Ben used his camera to get some **FTOGOAE**. ___FOOTAGE___

85. Alan had a strong **ULIPMSE** to buy some new shoes. _____

86. Jessie aimed the dart at the **TNCEER** of the board. _____

87. To strengthen his **LEUSCMS**, Omer frequently goes to the gym. _____

88. We watched the sun disappear over the **NOHRIOZ.** _____

89. Tameka's biggest **BAITMNOI** is to own a company. _____

90. Ally wanted to learn **GOREFIN** languages and travel the world. _____

91. The blizzard **EDIRHNED** Diego's effort to climb the mountain. _____

92. It was a **LIPVRIGEE** to enter the palace and meet the king. _____

93. Joshua apologised **ESCENILYR** for spilling juice on the floor. _____

94. Bethany **MUSAESD** the water fight was over, but she was wrong. _____

95. My team only had a **NUMEIT** chance of winning the game. _____

96. Nahla **WESRBOD** through the items in the catalogue. _____

Preparing for the Test

Thankfully, reading the dictionary isn't the only thing that will help you pass the VR part of the test...

Word Meanings Questions test your Vocabulary

Vocabulary means 'the set of words you know'. You can increase your vocabulary in a few ways:

1) Read lots of books and articles to help you learn new words.
2) Every time you come across a word you don't know, look it up in a dictionary and jot down the word and its definition in a notebook. Keep adding to the list and look over the words often.
3) Play word games such as SCRABBLE® or do crosswords to get you thinking about word meanings and how words are formed.
4) Do plenty of VR practice questions.

> It's important to read lots of different types of books: fiction, non-fiction and poetry as well as newspaper articles.

Practise spotting different Word Types

1) 'Word type' means what category a word belongs to — e.g. noun, verb, adjective or adverb.
2) Here are a few tips to help you work out the word types:

Nouns are people, places or things

1) Concrete nouns are objects and things. They can have 'a', 'an', 'the' or 'some' in front of them.

> a cow, an apple, the dog, some milk

2) Abstract nouns are harder to spot — they're things you can't see, hear, taste, touch or smell.
3) Abstract nouns can have 'my', 'his', 'her' or 'their' in front of them.

> my childhood, his freedom, her bravery

Verbs describe actions

1) A verb is a doing word.
2) Verbs can go after 'I', 'you', 'he', 'it', 'she' or 'they'.

> I play, you dance, they sing, it was

> Some words belong to more than one word type. E.g. 'I catch fish', 'there's a catch'. 'Catch' is a verb in the first sentence and a noun in the other.

Adverbs describe verbs

1) Adverbs add extra information — they tell you how, when, where or why an action is done.
2) Adverbs often end in -ly.

> quickly, happily, playfully

> Some adverbs can describe adjectives or other adverbs, e.g. "totally", "very", "quite".

Adjectives describe nouns

Adjectives sometimes end with -y, -ly, -ing.

> sandy, friendly, interesting

Preparing for the Test

Use **Word Type** to work out the **Answer**

Knowing and recognising word types can be a useful way of solving some questions in your VR test.

Put a word in a sentence to work out its **Word Type**

Sometimes a word may belong to more than one word type so you might be able to use it in a few different ways:

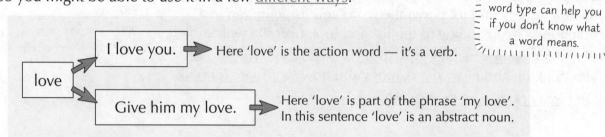

I love you. ➡ Here 'love' is the action word — it's a verb.

love

Give him my love. ➡ Here 'love' is part of the phrase 'my love'. In this sentence 'love' is an abstract noun.

> Being able to work out word type can help you if you don't know what a word means.

Look at word endings to help you work out **Word Type**

1) Sometimes you might need to find words that mean the same thing.
2) If you don't recognise some of the words, you could try looking at word type to help you.

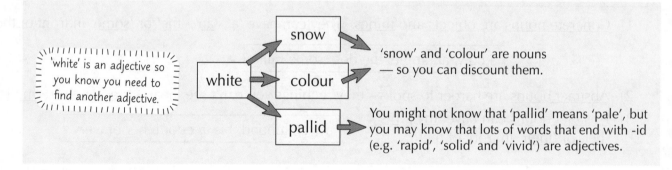

> 'white' is an adjective so you know you need to find another adjective.

white ➡ snow
white ➡ colour
white ➡ pallid

'snow' and 'colour' are nouns — so you can discount them.

You might not know that 'pallid' means 'pale', but you may know that lots of words that end with -id (e.g. 'rapid', 'solid' and 'vivid') are adjectives.

Practice Questions

1) Work out the word type of each of the following words:
   a) sang   c) nosy   e) cryptic   g) vacantly
   b) honesty   d) tighten   f) play   h) talent

2) Write down the meaning and word type of the following words.
   a) truth   b) cantankerous   c) wrathfully   d) bemusement

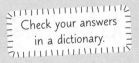
> Check your answers in a dictionary.

TEST TIP

There might be some words in the test that you don't know...

You'll recognise a lot of the words in the test, but there might be some tricky words in there to challenge you. If you come across a word you don't know, don't worry — try to eliminate as many of the other possible answers as you can, then make a sensible guess.

Closest Meaning

This question type is about synonyms — that's another way of saying 'words with similar meanings'.

11+ Example Question

Here's an <u>example</u> of the sort of question you might get in the <u>test</u>:

 **KEY EXAMPLE:** **Find two words, one from each set of brackets, that have the most similar meaning.**

(amble jog limp) (skip chase stroll)

- You need to pick <u>two words</u>, one from <u>each</u> set of brackets, that have the <u>closest meaning</u>.
- So the <u>answer</u> to this question is '<u>amble</u>' and '<u>stroll</u>' — both these words mean '<u>to walk slowly</u>'.

You need to know about **Synonyms** to answer these questions

1) Words with similar meanings are <u>synonyms</u> — e.g. small and tiny.
2) Pairs of synonyms are usually the <u>same</u> word type — e.g. <u>nouns</u>, <u>verbs</u>, <u>adjectives</u> or <u>adverbs</u>.

Some questions will try to **Catch You Out**

Make sure you pick the pair of words that <u>mean the same thing</u> — <u>don't</u> just pick two words that are <u>connected</u>.

(bucket well crate) (spade pail barrel)

You might pick 'bucket' and 'spade' — although they're connected, they don't mean the same thing. The right answer is 'bucket' and 'pail'.

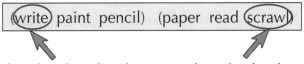

(write paint pencil) (paper read scrawl)

You might have heard 'read' and 'write' used together, but they don't mean the same thing. The right answer is 'write' and 'scrawl'.

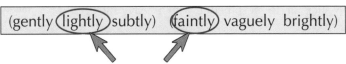

(gently lightly subtly) (faintly vaguely brightly)

'Light' and 'bright' can mean the same thing, but 'lightly' doesn't mean the same as 'brightly'. The right answer is 'faintly'.

 It may help you to picture the meaning of the words in your head so you can pick the pair that are the closest in meaning.

 **REVISION TIP** ## Double check your answers if you need to...

To check you've got the right answers, make up a sentence that uses your answer from the first set of brackets, then substitute in your answer from the second set. If the meaning of the sentence stays the same, then you've picked the right answers.

Closest Meaning

Use **Definitions** to help you answer the question

 **Find two words, one from each set of brackets, that have the most similar meaning.**

(glue stick fuse) (union team club)

Method 1 — Compare the meanings of words

1) Take the <u>first word</u> from the first set of brackets and think about its <u>meaning</u>.

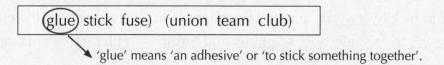

(glue) stick fuse) (union team club)

'glue' means 'an adhesive' or 'to stick something together'.

2) Compare its <u>meaning</u> with each word in the <u>second</u> set of brackets.

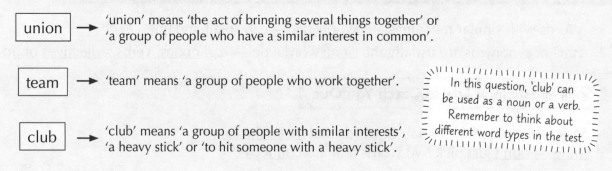

union → 'union' means 'the act of bringing several things together' or 'a group of people who have a similar interest in common'.

team → 'team' means 'a group of people who work together'.

club → 'club' means 'a group of people with similar interests', 'a heavy stick' or 'to hit someone with a heavy stick'.

In this question, 'club' can be used as a noun or a verb. Remember to think about different word types in the test.

3) <u>None</u> of these words have a meaning that's similar to '<u>glue</u>'.

4) So move on to the <u>second word</u> from the first bracket, and think about what it <u>means</u>.

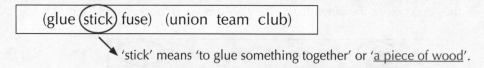

(glue (stick) fuse) (union team club)

'stick' means 'to glue something together' or '<u>a piece of wood</u>'.

5) This definition is <u>similar</u> to something we've seen <u>before</u>...

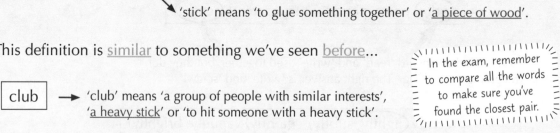

club → 'club' means 'a group of people with similar interests', '<u>a heavy stick</u>' or 'to hit someone with a heavy stick'.

In the exam, remember to compare all the words to make sure you've found the closest pair.

6) '<u>stick</u>' and '<u>club</u>' are very close in meaning — so this is the <u>answer</u>.

Connections might not be obvious straight away...

In the example above, the first set of words all mean 'to bind things together' and the second set all mean 'groups of people' — at first, there doesn't seem to be a connection between the two. If you get a question like this in the test, remember to think about alternative definitions for the words.

Closest Meaning

You can also look at **Word Type**

KEY EXAMPLE: **Find two words, one from each set of brackets, that have the most similar meaning.**

(chase rapidly competitive) (hasty immediate quickly)

> Take a look back at p.39 if you're not sure about word type.

Method 2 — Compare the word type

1) The correct pair will often be the <u>same type of word</u> — two nouns, two verbs etc. — as well as having the <u>same meaning</u>.

2) Start by looking at <u>word meaning</u> and <u>rule out</u> any words that don't mean the same thing.

(chase ~~chase~~ (rapidly) ~~competitive~~) ((hasty) ~~immediate~~ (quickly))

↳ You've narrowed the answers down to 'rapidly', 'hasty' and 'quickly' — they all mean 'doing things speedily'.

3) Take each word and <u>use it in a sentence</u> to help you work out the word type.

| He ate his dinner rapidly. | ✓ |
| He ate his dinner quickly. | ✓ |

'rapidly' and 'quickly' both end in -ly and can be used in the same way. They're the same word type — adverbs.

| He ate his dinner hasty. | ✗ |

'hasty' can't be used in the same way as the other two words. It also ends in -y, which helps you to work out that it's an adjective.

4) By looking at the <u>meaning</u> and the <u>word type</u>, you can work out that '<u>rapidly</u>' and '<u>quickly</u>' have the <u>closest meaning</u>.

Practice Questions

Find two words, one from each set of brackets, that have the most similar meaning.

1) (afraid scary menacing)   (aghast shocked terrified)

2) (stride traipse trail)   (rambler track tread)

3) (smiled laughed chuckled)   (grimaced happily beamed)

Always read the question wording carefully.

TEST TIP

In the test, you could also be asked to find words with **opposite** meanings (p.44-46). These questions will be in the same format as Closest Meaning questions, so be sure to read the instructions carefully to make sure you answer the question in the right way.

Opposite Meaning

The opposite of good is bad. The opposite of night is day. The opposite of synonym is antonym.

11+ Example Question

Here's an <u>example</u> of the sort of question you might get in the real thing:

 **Find two words, one from each set of brackets, that have the most opposite meaning.**

(clean new fresh) (messy filthy dreary)

- Pick <u>two words</u>, one from <u>each</u> set of brackets that are the <u>most different</u> in meaning.
- The answer is '<u>clean</u>' and '<u>filthy</u>' because 'filthy' means 'dirty' which is the opposite of '<u>clean</u>'.

This question is asking about **Antonyms**

1) Words that have <u>opposite meanings</u> are called <u>antonyms</u> — e.g. 'new' and 'old'.
2) Here are some more examples of <u>antonyms</u>:

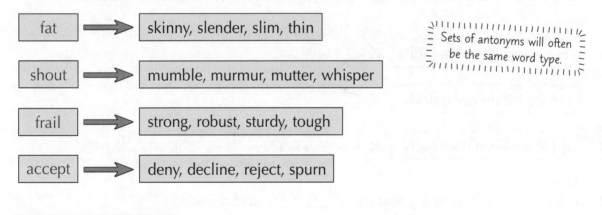

fat	→	skinny, slender, slim, thin
shout	→	mumble, murmur, mutter, whisper
frail	→	strong, robust, sturdy, tough
accept	→	deny, decline, reject, spurn

Sets of antonyms will often be the same word type.

Look at the **Prefixes**

You can turn some words into <u>antonyms</u> by adding certain <u>prefixes</u> such as <u>un-</u>, <u>dis-</u> or <u>in-</u>.

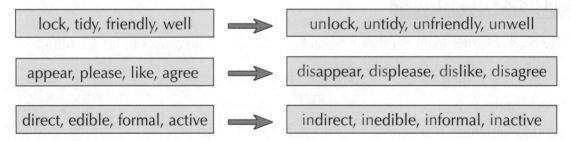

lock, tidy, friendly, well	→	unlock, untidy, unfriendly, unwell
appear, please, like, agree	→	disappear, displease, dislike, disagree
direct, edible, formal, active	→	indirect, inedible, informal, inactive

---

REVISION TIP

Practice makes perfect... inaction makes imperfect...

If you want to practise thinking of antonyms, open your favourite book and choose a paragraph. Read through the paragraph, writing down all of the verbs, adjectives and adverbs that you find. Then, jot down as many antonyms as you can think of for each one.

Opposite Meaning

Use **Definitions** to help you answer the question

 **KEY EXAMPLE:** **Find two words, one from each set of brackets, that have the most opposite meaning.**

(sometimes frequently usually) (rarely constantly habitually)

You can use a similar method for the opposite and closest meanings questions.

Method 1 — Compare the meanings of words

1) Take the <u>first word</u> from the first set of brackets and think about its <u>meaning</u>.

((sometimes) frequently usually) (rarely constantly habitually)

'sometimes' means 'every now and then'.

2) Compare its <u>meaning</u> with each word in the <u>second</u> set of brackets.

rarely → 'rarely' means 'not often'.

constantly → 'constantly' means 'continuing without pause'.

habitually → 'habitually' means 'frequently'.

Remember, you have to pick a word from each set of brackets.

3) <u>None</u> of these words have a meaning that's <u>directly opposite</u> to '<u>sometimes</u>'.

4) So move on to the <u>second word</u> from the first bracket, and think about what it <u>means</u>.

(sometimes (frequently) usually) (rarely constantly habitually)

'frequently' means '<u>often</u>'.

5) This definition means the <u>opposite</u> to something we've seen <u>before</u>...

rarely → 'rarely' means '<u>not often</u>'.

In the exam, remember to compare all the words to make sure you've found the words with the most opposite meaning.

6) '<u>frequently</u>' and '<u>rarely</u>' are almost <u>opposites</u> — so that's your <u>answer</u>.

Test out your answer by putting it in a sentence...

Sometimes there might be another pair of words that seems like a possible answer, for example 'sometimes' and 'constantly' in the example above. The trick here is to think carefully about what each word means (trying both words in the same sentence may help you, e.g. "I swim sometimes" and "I swim constantly") and to pick the pair of words that are the most opposite in meaning.

Opposite Meaning

Narrow Down the options and use Word Type to find the answer

 **KEY EXAMPLE:** **Find two words, one from each set of brackets, that have the most opposite meaning.**

(enemy hostage release) (unlock capture captivity)

Method 2 — Compare the word type

1) <u>Read</u> the question. <u>Think</u> about the meanings of the words and <u>rule out</u> any words that don't have <u>antonyms</u> in the question.

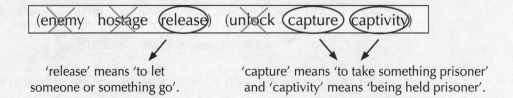

'release' means 'to let someone or something go'.

'capture' means 'to take something prisoner' and 'captivity' means 'being held prisoner'.

2) Once you've <u>narrowed down</u> your options, think about the remaining words — the answers will often be the <u>same word type</u>.

3) Take each word and <u>use it in a sentence</u> to help you work out the word type.

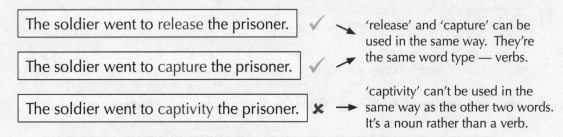

The soldier went to release the prisoner. ✓

The soldier went to capture the prisoner. ✓

'release' and 'capture' can be used in the same way. They're the same word type — verbs.

The soldier went to captivity the prisoner. ✗

'captivity' can't be used in the same way as the other two words. It's a noun rather than a verb.

4) By looking at the <u>meaning</u> and the <u>word type</u>, we can work out that '<u>release</u>' and '<u>capture</u>' are the <u>most opposite</u> in meaning.

Practice Questions

Find two words, one from each set of brackets, that have the most opposite meaning.

1) (absent blank vacant)   (present available missing)
2) (claim accuse argue)   (protect guard defend)
3) (abolish hinder renounce) (endure establish extend)

REVISION TIP

Don't forget words can have more than one meaning...

Some words belong to more than one word type, so consider the different meanings of the word. For example, the noun 'fly' refers to an insect, but the verb can mean 'to soar'.

Multiple Meanings

These questions are on homographs — that's 'a word with more than one meaning' to you and me.

11+ Example Question

Take a look at this 11+ sample question:

 **Choose the word that has a similar meaning to the words in both sets of brackets.**

(sphere globe) (dance party)   orb spin ball gala circle

- You need to pick <u>one</u> of the five options which has the <u>same meaning</u> as the <u>words in brackets</u>.
- So the answer is '<u>ball</u>' because it can mean both '<u>a sphere or globe</u>' and '<u>a dance or party</u>'.

You need to be able to recognise **Homographs** for this question

Homographs have the **Same Spelling**

<u>Homographs</u> are words that have the <u>same spelling</u> but <u>different meanings</u>:

| My watch is an hour fast. | I watch TV after dinner. |

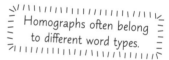
Homographs often belong to different word types.

The word 'watch' has two different meanings in these sentences.
You only know which meaning it is by reading the rest of the sentence.

Some homographs are **Pronounced Differently**

Some homographs have the <u>same spelling</u>, but are <u>pronounced differently</u>:

| A female pig is a sow. | The farmer was going to sow her seeds. |

The word 'sow' has two different meanings in these sentences.
They're also pronounced differently, but they're both spelt the same.

 ## Think about words from different angles...

If you're stuck on a Multiple Meanings question when you're revising, try writing as many sentences as you can using the words in brackets. Think about whether each word can be used as a noun, verb, adjective or adverb, or as more than one of these word types.

Multiple Meanings

Work through each word **One By One**

 **Choose the word that has a similar meaning to the words in both sets of brackets.**

(greet salute) (sleet snow)   wave rain bow hail storm

Method 1 — Rule out the wrong options

1) <u>Read</u> through the words in the <u>brackets</u>.

2) Think about what both sets <u>mean</u>.

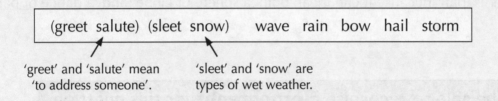

(greet salute) (sleet snow)   wave rain bow hail storm

'greet' and 'salute' mean 'to address someone'.

'sleet' and 'snow' are types of wet weather.

3) Take a look at the five options and try to <u>rule out</u> any possible answers.

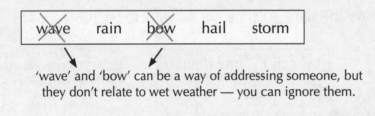

wave rain bow hail storm

'wave' and 'bow' can be a way of addressing someone, but they don't relate to wet weather — you can ignore them.

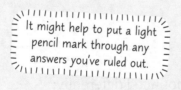 It might help to put a light pencil mark through any answers you've ruled out.

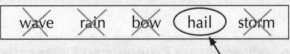

wave rain bow (hail) storm

'rain' and 'storm' are types of wet weather, but they don't mean 'to address or salute'. That leaves us with 'hail'.

4) <u>Check</u> your answer by using the word in <u>two sentences</u> — one for <u>each meaning</u>.

| The weather forecast predicted hail. | ✓ |

| All hail the new king. | ✓ |

Don't worry if you don't know a word...

If you don't recognise one of the words in a set of brackets, you can still answer the question. The other word in that set will mean the same thing, so work with the word you do know.

Multiple Meanings

Try putting the words into a **Sentence**

KEY EXAMPLE: (waft blow) (admirer devotee)   supporter follower breeze fan gust

Method 2 — Use each word in a sentence

1) <u>Read</u> through the question. <u>Think</u> about what the words in the brackets <u>mean</u>.

'waft' and 'blow' both mean 'to move air'. →   (waft blow) (admirer devotee) ← 'admirer' and 'devotee' mean someone who is enthusiastic about something.

2) Take the <u>first set</u> of brackets, and <u>rule out</u> any answers that don't <u>match</u> that <u>definition</u>.

(waft blow) (admirer devotee) supporter ✗ follower ✗ breeze fan gust

'supporter' and 'follower' don't have anything to do with moving air.

3) Take the <u>second set</u> of brackets and use one of the words in a <u>sensible sentence</u>.

(admirer devotee) → I'm a devotee of Ulverston United football club.

4) Take <u>each</u> of the <u>remaining</u> possible answers and use them in the <u>same sentence</u>. There should only be <u>one word</u> that <u>makes sense</u> in the <u>same sentence</u> — that's the <u>answer</u>.

I'm a breeze of Ulverston United football club. ✗

I'm a fan of Ulverston United football club. ✓

I'm a gust of Ulverston United football club. ✗

5) The answer is '<u>fan</u>' because it matches the definitions for <u>both</u> sets of words.

Practice Questions

Choose the word that has a similar meaning to the words in both sets of brackets.

1) (lecture discussion) (chat natter)   speak   talk   project   articulate   speech
2) (manage supervise) (sprint dash)   boss   jog   rush   run   oversee
3) (schedule reserve) (novel text)   story   book   organise   arrange   manual

 TEST TIP

Try to give an answer for every question...

If you've narrowed down the options but you've still got more than one possible answer left, don't just leave the answer blank — a sensible guess is better than no answer at all.

Odd Ones Out

The best way to prepare for Odd Ones Out questions is to make sure your vocabulary is top-notch...

11+ Example Question

Here's an example of the sort of question you might get in the test:

 **Three of the words in the list are linked. Mark the two words that are not related to these three.**

whisper   bellow   murmur   mutter   exclaim

- You need to pick two of the five words that isn't connected to the other three.
- The answers are 'bellow' and 'exclaim' because the rest of the words describe speaking quietly.

Use Word Meaning to find the answer

 **Three of the words in the list are linked. Mark the two words that are not related to these three.**

steal   borrow   lend   contribute   snatch

Method 1 — Compare the meanings of words

1) Read through all the words. Think about what each word means.

steal	→ 'steal' means 'to take something without permission'.
borrow	→ 'borrow' means 'to take something temporarily'.
lend	→ 'lend' means 'to give something temporarily'.
contribute	→ 'contribute' means 'to give or supply something'.
snatch	→ 'snatch' means 'to take something suddenly'.

This question is testing your ability to define words.

2) Try to make a connection between three of the words.

The odd ones out won't always be connected to each other — they just have to be unrelated to the other three.

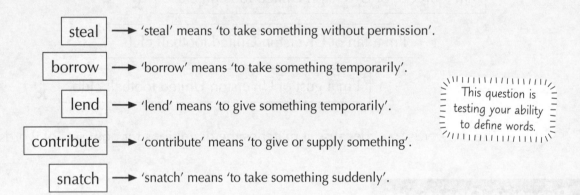

steal   borrow   ⊘lend⊘   ⊘contribute⊘   snatch

'steal', 'borrow' and 'snatch' all mean 'to take' — 'lend' and 'contribute' mean 'to give'.

3) The odd ones out are 'lend' and 'contribute' — so that's your answer.

Odd Ones Out

Use Word Type to find the answer

KEY EXAMPLE: **Three of the words in the list are linked. Mark the two words that are <u>not</u> related to these three.**

blemish   error   wrongly   flaw   mark

Method 2 — Compare the word type

1) Sometimes you might get a list of words that have <u>similar meanings</u>. To solve these types of questions it might help to think about <u>word type</u>.

2) <u>Read</u> through all the words. Think about the <u>word type</u> of each word.

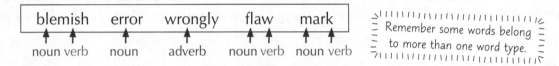

Remember some words belong to more than one word type.

3) <u>Identify</u> any word types that <u>don't match</u> the others. So in this question, 'wrongly' is <u>one half</u> of the <u>answer</u>.

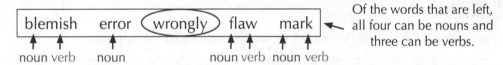

Of the words that are left, all four can be nouns and three can be verbs.

4) Try and make a <u>connection</u> between <u>three</u> of the words.

blemish   error   flaw   ← 'Blemish' and 'flaw' both mean 'an imperfection' or 'to make an imperfection'. 'Error' means 'something misguided or incorrect'.

'Mark' can mean 'a score' or 'to give a score', but it can also mean 'an imperfection' or 'to make an imperfection'.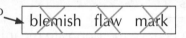

5) 'Blemish', 'flaw' and 'mark' are <u>synonyms</u>, so '<u>wrongly</u>' and '<u>error</u>' are the <u>odd ones out</u>.

Practice Questions

Three of the words in each list are linked. Mark the two words that are not related to these three.

1) calm   peaceful   dull   dreary   tedious
2) poem   biography   recipe   newspaper   novel
3) lethargic   drowsy   slumbering   listless   dormant

Make sure you know your nouns...

REVISION TIP — If you're given a group of five nouns and you're struggling to work out which two are the odd ones out, try thinking about the nature or purpose of the object or thing that each noun refers to. This will help you to spot the options that don't fit with the others.

Word Connections

Word Connections questions look a bit complex but they're less scary once you know the tricks...

11+ Example Question

Take a look at this <u>11+ style question</u> — you might get something like this in the test:

> **Choose two words, one from each set of brackets, that complete the sentence in the most sensible way.**
>
> **Red** is to (pink colour paint) as **eight** is to (spider age number).

- You need to make a <u>connection</u> between one word from <u>each set of brackets</u> and the <u>words in bold</u>. Both pairs of words should be <u>linked in the same way</u>.
- So the answers are '<u>colour</u>' and '<u>number</u>' because <u>red</u> is a colour and <u>eight</u> is a number.

Words can be linked in **Different Ways**

Synonyms

The answers have the <u>same definition</u> as the words in the question.

> **Silly** is to (joke foolish clown) as **sensible** is to (teacher boring reasonable).

In this example, 'foolish' is a synonym of 'silly', and 'reasonable' is a synonym of 'sensible'.

Antonyms

The answers have the <u>opposite meaning</u> to the words in the question.

> **Calm** is to (ocean frenzied serene) as **happy** is to (sad family birthday).

Here, 'calm' is an antonym of 'frenzied', and 'happy' is an antonym of 'sad'.

Context

Sometimes the question might test your <u>general knowledge</u>.

> **Cue** is to (actor traffic snooker) as **racket** is to (noisy tennis sport).

To answer this question, you need to know that snooker players use cues and tennis players use rackets.

Exercise is to fitness as practice is to success...

It might be tricky to find the links between words at first, but the more you practise answering these questions, the quicker you'll get at spotting the sort of connections that might be in the test.

Word Connections

Think of Links between the words

Choose two words, one from each set of brackets, that complete the sentence in the most sensible way.

Horse is to (foal field bridle) as **swan** is to (bird feather cygnet).

Method 1 — Compare the meanings

1) Take the first word and think about its meaning.

A horse is an animal that can be ridden, and that lives in fields or on farms. ← (Horse) is to (foal field bridle)

2) Take a look at the words in the first bracket and try and link them to 'horse'.

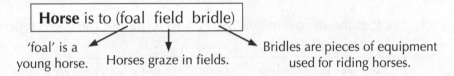

Horse is to (foal field bridle)

'foal' is a young horse.   Horses graze in fields.   Bridles are pieces of equipment used for riding horses.

3) Think about the meaning of the second word.

A swan is a bird that lives in fresh water. ← (swan) is to (bird feather cygnet).

4) Look at the words in the second bracket. Think about what links them to 'swan'.

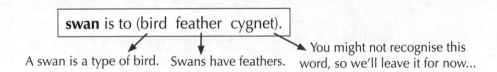

swan is to (bird feather cygnet).

A swan is a type of bird.   Swans have feathers.   You might not recognise this word, so we'll leave it for now...

5) Try to eliminate any words that definitely aren't right.

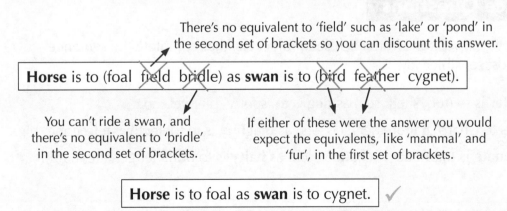

There's no equivalent to 'field' such as 'lake' or 'pond' in the second set of brackets so you can discount this answer.

Horse is to (foal field bridle) as **swan** is to (bird feather cygnet).

You can't ride a swan, and there's no equivalent to 'bridle' in the second set of brackets.   If either of these were the answer you would expect the equivalents, like 'mammal' and 'fur', in the first set of brackets.

Horse is to foal as **swan** is to cygnet. ✓

6) 'Cygnet' is the name for a baby swan. This example shows that if you come across a word you don't know you shouldn't panic. Just work around it as much as you can.

Word Connections

Use **Word Types** to help you

 **KEY EXAMPLE:** Choose two words, one from each set of brackets, that complete the sentence in the most sensible way.

Fearless is to (soldier intrepid bravely) as **cowardly** is to (idle fled timid).

Method 2 — Compare the word type

1) If the words have similar meanings it might help to think about their word type.

2) Read the question. If you can, rule out any answers that don't have a connection.

> **Fearless** is to (soldier intrepid bravely) as **cowardly** is to (i̶d̶l̶e̶ fled timid).

'idle' means 'lazy' and doesn't have any connection to 'cowardly'.

3) Look at the remaining words. Try to work out the word type of each word.

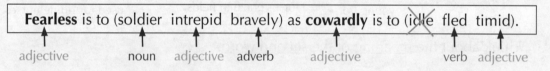

> **Fearless** is to (soldier intrepid bravely) as **cowardly** is to (i̶d̶l̶e̶ fled timid).
>   adjective   noun   adjective adverb   adjective   verb adjective

4) Try to spot a link between the word types. In this example, both 'fearless' and 'cowardly' are adjectives, and there's a matching adjective in each of the brackets — 'intrepid' and 'timid'.

5) Double check your answer makes sense by reading it through.

> **Fearless** is to intrepid as **cowardly** is to timid. ✓

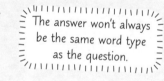 The answer won't always be the same word type as the question.

Practice Questions

Choose two words, one from each set of brackets, that complete the sentence in the most sensible way.

1) **Lobster** is to (red shell sea) as **dog** is to (spotty blanket coat).
2) **Cut** is to (sharp hairdresser scissors) as **magnify** is to (detective telescope big).
3) **Fortunate** is to (unlucky chance rich) as **hairy** is to (follicle genetic bald).

 ## Make every second count...

In the test, don't waste time writing word types in full — abbreviate verb to 'V' and noun to 'N'. Don't get adjectives and adverbs mixed up — use 'Aj' and 'Av' to make it clear.

Reorder Words to Make a Sentence

Reorder the sentence in this words and halfway you're there...

11+ Example Question

Here's an example of the kind of <u>question</u> you might be asked in the <u>test</u>:

 **Find the two words that should be swapped in order for this sentence to make sense.**

I'm going on December in holiday.

- You need to swap a <u>pair</u> of words in the sentence so that it makes <u>sense</u>.
- The answer is '<u>December</u>' and '<u>holiday</u>' — the sentence is 'I'm going on <u>holiday</u> in <u>December</u>'.

Pick Out the words that don't Sound Right

 **Find the two words that should be swapped in order for this sentence to make sense.**

The burned microwave old my dinner.

Method 1 — Identify the part that sounds wrong

1) Read through the sentence and <u>identify</u> the part that <u>doesn't sound right</u>.

> The <u>burned microwave old</u> my dinner.

There's something funny going on here...

2) Once you've identified the bit that doesn't make sense, try <u>switching a pair</u> of words around.

> The microwave burned <u>old my</u> dinner.

'burned' and 'microwave' have been swapped...   ... but this bit still doesn't sound right.

3) If your new sentence still doesn't sound right, go back to the <u>original sentence</u> and try switching <u>another pair of words</u>.

4) Once you're happy, check that the sentence <u>sounds right</u>.

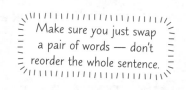
Make sure you just swap a pair of words — don't reorder the whole sentence.

> The old microwave burned my dinner. ✓

This sounds more like it.

Reorder Words to Make a Sentence

You can also look at Word Types

 **EXAMPLE:** **Find the two words that should be swapped in order for this sentence to make sense.**

Jo girl the happiest is I know.

Method 2 — Compare the word type

1) Read the sentence. If you can't spot the words to swap straight away, read the sentence again and identify the part that doesn't sound right.

Jo girl the happiest is I know.

2) This time, look at the position of different word types in the sentence.

Jo girl the happiest is I know.

There are two nouns here.   There are two verbs here.

It looks like there are too many nouns at the start of the sentence and too many verbs at the end.

3) When you swap a pair of words, check that the tenses match and that they agree.

'Jo know' doesn't sound right — the verb and noun don't agree. It should be 'Jo knows'.

Jo know the happiest is I girl.

The rest of the sentence sounds wrong too.

4) Swap the words until the sentence makes sense and it's grammatically correct.

The noun 'Jo' and the verb 'is' agree.

Jo is the happiest girl I know. ✓

Practice Questions

Find the two words that should be swapped for each sentence to make sense.

1) Quickly the footpath if you want to get there take.
2) My Fluffy has a pet Beagle called Nan.
3) The bolts had silver robot and blue wires.
4) It's my birthday week a today.

 ## Read, read and read some more...

It'll really help you in the test if you're familiar with how sentences are constructed — reading lots of books, newspapers and magazines can help you build this understanding.

Practice Questions

That's nearly it for the Word Meanings section — now it's time to practise what you've learnt. If you're struggling with a question, go back and recap the methods that you can use to answer it.

Closest Meaning

> Underline two words, one from each set of brackets, that have the most similar meaning. Look at this example:
>
> **Example:**   (sombre <u>drab</u> bare)   (harsh loose <u>dull</u>)

1. (steal   clasp   steady)   (tighten   capture   clutch)

2. (relentless   abrupt   intense)   (impatient   continuous   furious)

3. (expel   overthrow   counter)   (oppose   back   deny)

4. (function   quality   style)   (ability   technique   qualification)

5. (line   range   border)   (extent   zone   segment)

6. (prohibit   delay   obstruct)   (sedate   detain   cancel)

7. (situate   lower   crouch)   (stoop   compress   perch)

8. (detailed   rigid   lavish)   (exhaustive   copious   precise)

9. (portion   particle   form)   (dosage   entity   granule)

10. (forward   arrogant   poised)   (dominant   bold   discourteous)

11. (disable   reserve   withdraw)   (invert   bestow   retract)

12. (linger   roam   occupy)   (loiter   inhibit   amble)

Practice Questions

Opposite Meaning

Underline two words, one from each set of brackets, that have the most opposite meaning. Look at this example:

Example: (stained <u>smooth</u> glaring) (dirty <u>coarse</u> light)

13. (unsettle expose disturb)   (deceive uncover conceal)

14. (approach subside near)   (recede evade conclude)

15. (shield conflict resist)   (conserve protect harmony)

16. (special creative unusual)   (belated routine ordered)

17. (faded flushed discoloured)   (tarnished ashen serene)

18. (overjoyed grateful fulfilled)   (nonchalant exasperated devastated)

19. (subordinate adviser ally)   (bystander adversary accomplice)

20. (drastic inessential possible)   (urgent decisive imperative)

21. (remote uncommon odd)   (prevalent foreign exceptional)

22. (premature mistimed quick)   (hasty overdue foreseeable)

23. (pressure coax encourage)   (disapprove dispirit disengage)

24. (forgotten current immediate)   (obsolete disregarded exhausted)

Practice Questions

Multiple Meanings

Choose the word that has a similar meaning to the words in both sets of brackets. Underline your answer. Look at this example:

Example: (delicacy luxury) (cure heal)   <u>treat</u> aid delight care mend

25. **(institution academy)** **(educate teach)**   school college tutor learn class

26. **(question challenge)** **(face tackle)**   ambush confront strike accost dare

27. **(hint suggestion)**   **(murmur mutter)**   sign mumble secret idea whisper

28. **(bright brilliant)**   **(kindle ignite)**   light spark intelligent glow shine

29. **(effort trouble)**   **(harass annoy)**   plague pest bother irk tease

30. **(obscured confused)** **(murky overcast)**   blurred eclipsed bleak clouded dim

31. **(lacking needing)**   **(lost mislaid)**   away deficient limited missing gone

32. **(provide give)**   **(present submit)**   transfer donate offer afford gift

33. **(enclosure paddock)** **(write compose)**   draft coop scribble pen compound

34. **(miracle marvel)**   **(awe amazement)** oddity revere dread shock wonder

35. **(deserve warrant)**   **(virtue benefit)**   earn reward desire justify merit

36. **(construct make)**   **(figure shape)**   produce physique build sort fashion

Practice Questions

Odd Ones Out

Three of the words in each list are linked. Underline the two
words that are not related to these three. Look at this example:

Example: wind   gale   <u>shower</u>   hurricane   <u>sleet</u>

37. subordinate   chief   counterpart   director   chairperson

38. jump   lifting   hurdle   rise   increase

39. lament   complain   mourn   blame   grieve

40. remedy   affliction   disorder   therapy   condition

41. discipline   speciality   restraint   willpower   talent

42. lump   shred   morsel   slab   chunk

43. repel   repulse   defeat   vanquish   disgust

44. futile   barren   yielding   ineffectual   fruitless

45. unspoken   hushed   wordless   mute   discreet

46. cut   graze   slash   chafe   lacerate

47. expertise   proficiency   professional   prowess   judgement

48. resistance   concern   timidity   apprehension   uneasiness

Practice Questions

Word Connections

Choose two words, one from each set of brackets, that complete the sentence in the most sensible way. Underline both words.
Look at this example.

Example: Pearl is to (sea <u>oyster</u> jewel) as **pip** is to (plant grow <u>apple</u>).

49. **Pane** is to (look window square) as **panel** is to (wood part door).

50. **Historical** is to (date artefact past) as **modern** is to (current future technology).

51. **Deep** is to (chasm bottom shallow) as **expansive** is to (restricted far length).

52. **Navigator** is to (search map find) as **scientist** is to (job microscope laboratory).

53. **Pear** is to (tree branch fruit) as **gooseberry** is to (crumble leaf bush).

54. **Amber** is to (mineral resin fire) as **turquoise** is to (precious blue ocean).

55. **Forage** is to (hunt find food) as **learn** is to (reading knowledge think).

56. **Bloom** is to (spring flourish leaf) as **wither** is to (shrivel debris flower).

57. **Nostalgia** is to (photo memory time) as **satisfaction** is to (success glad try).

58. **Expensive** is to (money affordable luxury) as **rich** is to (mansion destitute gold).

59. **Hall** is to (corridor house narrow) as **lobby** is to (entrance waiting hotel).

60. **Potato** is to (skin chips roast) as **orange** is to (fruit rind colour).

Practice Questions

Reorder Words to Make a Sentence

Find two words which should be swapped in order for each sentence to make sense. Underline both words. Look at this example:

Example: The waiter carried the <u>kitchen</u> into the <u>dessert</u>.

61. The experienced astronaut inside floats happily her spaceship.

62. The every athletes run ten miles dedicated other day.

63. She generously bouquet me a beautiful gave of flowers.

64. I am definitely one to travel around the world going day.

65. My oldest in is a respected soldier step-sister the army.

66. Mateo fluently speak both Spanish and English can.

67. Our rusty the broke down at the side of car motorway.

68. I went skydiving were we when holidaying in Thailand last year.

69. The along rat scampered curious the empty street at night.

70. Kalifa has second finished writing her almost fantasy novel.

71. He is tonight to bake a giant chocolate cake later planning.

72. Joe tripped when he suddenly exclaimed over the protruding rock.

Preparing for the Test

You just can't escape maths — it pops up everywhere, even in Verbal Reasoning...

Get used to doing maths **Without** a **Calculator**

1) You won't be allowed a calculator in your test, so you need to be able to do all the maths in your head or on paper.

2) Writing sums out on paper takes time — try and do as much as you can in your head. Here are some ideas to help you practise:

> * Do the maths-based puzzles in a puzzle magazine.
> * Play board games that test your maths skills.
> * Practise lots of different VR questions.

3) You'll have to work through sums with up to four steps, but these will only use addition, subtraction, multiplication and division:

$$8 + 4 = 12 \qquad 8 - 4 = 4 \qquad 8 \times 4 = 32 \qquad 8 \div 4 = 2$$

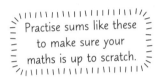

Practise sums like these to make sure your maths is up to scratch.

Practise your **Times Tables**

1) Knowing your times tables will help you recognise factors and multiples, which are important in lots of the Maths and Sequences questions.

Factors

Factors are the numbers you can divide another number by to get a whole number. The factors of 12 are:

$$12 \div 1 = 12 \qquad 12 \div 2 = 6 \qquad 12 \div 3 = 4$$

$$12 \div 4 = 3 \qquad 12 \div 6 = 2 \qquad 12 \div 12 = 1$$

So 12 has six factors: 1, 2, 3, 4, 6 and 12.

Multiples

Multiples are the numbers you get when you multiply a whole number by another whole number. Some multiples of 3 are:

$$3 \times 1 = 3 \qquad 3 \times 2 = 6 \qquad 3 \times 3 = 9 \qquad 3 \times 4 = 12$$

$$3 \times 5 = 15 \qquad 3 \times 6 = 18 \qquad 3 \times 7 = 21 \qquad 3 \times 8 = 24$$

So any number in the three times table is a multiple of 3.

2) Practise with a friend by taking it in turns to test each other on your times tables. Test yourself by making times table flashcards with the answer on the back.

Preparing for the Test

Think **Logically** for **Sequence Questions**

1) <u>Sequence</u> questions involve spotting <u>patterns</u> in the <u>jumps</u> between <u>numbers</u> or <u>letters</u>.

2) These jumps could be <u>alternating numbers</u>, <u>increasing</u> or <u>decreasing</u> numbers, <u>even</u> numbers etc.

3) You need to work out the <u>pattern</u> and think about what the <u>logical next step</u> would be.

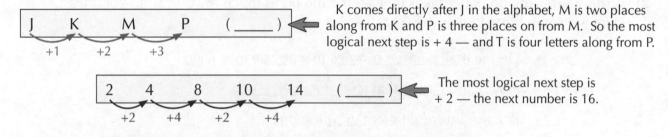

K comes directly after J in the alphabet, M is two places along from K and P is three places on from M. So the most logical next step is + 4 — and T is four letters along from P.

The most logical next step is + 2 — the next number is 16.

Sequences can be based on **Square numbers** or **Fibonacci numbers**

1) <u>Square numbers</u> are the numbers you get when you <u>multiply a number by itself</u>. Here are the first few:

| $1 \times 1 = 1$ | $2 \times 2 = 4$ | $3 \times 3 = 9$ | $4 \times 4 = 16$ | $5 \times 5 = 25$ |

Prime numbers (numbers that are only divisible by themselves and 1) could come up too.

2) <u>Fibonacci sequences</u> are strings of numbers where <u>the two previous numbers</u> are <u>added together</u> to get the <u>next number</u> in the sequence. Here's an example:

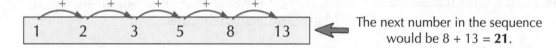

The next number in the sequence would be 8 + 13 = **21**.

Knowing the **Alphabet** will help you work **Quickly**

Make sure you <u>know the alphabet</u> really well before the test. You'll often have to <u>count</u> along it or use it to find <u>patterns</u> in <u>Letter Sequences</u> questions.

The Alphabet Circle

1) For some Verbal Reasoning questions you'll need to <u>count backwards</u> from **A** to **Z** or <u>count on</u> from **Z** to **A**.

2) This is easier if you imagine the <u>alphabet</u> as a <u>continuous circle</u> — you can just keep <u>counting around the circle</u>.

3) For example, you can use it to find the <u>next letter</u> in this <u>sequence</u>:

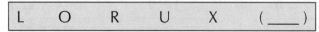

4) Use the <u>alphabet circle</u> to find the pattern — in this question you move <u>forward 3 letters each time</u>.

5) When you reach the <u>end</u> of the <u>alphabet</u>, use the <u>alphabet circle</u> to <u>continue counting</u>. This will help you work out that the <u>letter</u> after <u>X</u> is <u>A</u>.

You'll be given an alphabet line for some questions in the test.

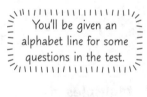

Complete the Sum

Don't be afraid of Complete the Sum questions — they're easier than they look.

11+ Example Question

Here's an <u>example</u> of the sort of question you might get in the <u>test</u>:

 **KEY EXAMPLE:** **Find the missing number to complete the sum.**

$$5 \times 4 + 3 - 6 = (\underline{})$$

- You need to find the number that <u>fills the gap</u> so that the <u>right hand side</u> of the sum is <u>equal to</u> the <u>left hand side</u>.

- The answer is <u>17</u> — <u>5</u> multiplied by <u>4</u> equals <u>20</u>. If you add <u>3</u> to <u>20</u> then you get <u>23</u>. If you subtract <u>6</u> from <u>23</u>, you get <u>17</u>.

Work Through the questions One Step at a time

 **KEY EXAMPLE:** **Find the missing number to complete the sum.**

$$15 \div 3 + 9 - 2 = (\underline{})$$

Method 1 — Write the answer down as you go

1) <u>Complete the Sum</u> questions often have <u>more than one step</u>.

2) Look at the <u>sum</u> and work out the <u>answer</u> to the <u>first step</u>.

$$\boxed{(15 \div 3) + 9 - 2 = (\underline{})} \longrightarrow \boxed{15 \div 3 = 5}$$

3) Then use the answer in the <u>second step</u>.

$$\boxed{5 + 9 = 14}$$

> Write down the answer to each step as you go along so you don't get confused.

4) Finally use that answer in the <u>third step</u>.

$$\boxed{14 - 2 = 12}$$

5) This is the <u>last step</u> in the sum, so the answer to the <u>sum</u> is <u>12</u>.

 ## Revise your times tables...

Make sure you know your times tables inside out before the test. This will make it a lot quicker for you to do the multiplications and divisions in the maths questions in the test.

Complete the Sum

Work on **One Half** of the sum at a time

Find the missing number to complete the sum.

$$24 \div 6 + 19 = 16 + (\_\_\_\_)$$

Method 2 — Break the sum into two halves

1) Break the sum into <u>two halves</u> either side of the equals sign.

$$24 \div 6 + 19 = 16 + (\_\_\_\_)$$

$$24 \div 6 + 19 = ?$$ $$? = 16 + (\_\_\_\_)$$

2) <u>Start</u> with the <u>sum</u> which has <u>all its numbers</u> — this is <u>usually the left hand sum</u>.

3) Break the sum down into <u>steps</u> and do each step <u>in order</u>:

$$24 \div 6 = 4$$ ←   This is where knowing your times tables is handy.

$$4 + 19 = 23$$ ←   This next step is simple addition. <u>Write it down</u> if you need to.

4) Now you know that the <u>answer</u> to the <u>left hand sum</u> is <u>23</u>.

5) The <u>answer</u> to the <u>right hand sum</u> has to <u>equal</u> the answer to the <u>left hand sum</u>. You need to find a number that will <u>fill the gap</u> and make the <u>right hand sum</u> equal <u>23</u> too.

$$23 = 16 + (\_\_\_\_)$$

6) To <u>fill in the last gap</u>, you need to find the <u>number</u> that you can <u>add to 16</u> to make <u>23</u>. To do that, you need to <u>subtract</u> 16 from 23 to work out the <u>difference</u> between them.

$$23 - 16 = 7$$ → $$23 = 16 + (\underline{\ 7\ })$$ So the complete sum looks like this. → $$24 \div 6 + 19 = 16 + (\underline{\ 7\ })$$

Practice Questions

Find the missing number to complete the sum.

1) $11 \times 4 = 24 + (\_\_\_\_)$

2) $30 - 4 = 19 + (\_\_\_\_)$

3) $54 \div 9 = 2 + (\_\_\_\_)$

4) $18 \div 3 \times 2 + 4 = 10 + (\_\_\_\_)$

TEST TIP

Make sure to mark the correct answer in the test...

Be careful when you're marking your answer for Complete the Sum questions in the test. The answer is the number that fills the gap in the sum, not the answer to both sums.

Letter Sequences

Letter Sequences can be tricky, but with a bit of practice they'll be a piece of cake.

11+ Example Question

You might be asked questions like this one in the test:

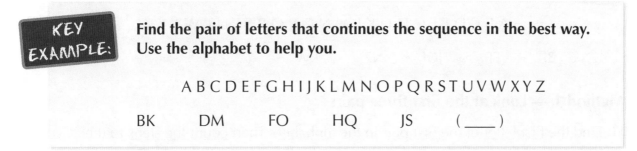

KEY EXAMPLE:
Find the pair of letters that continues the sequence in the best way.
Use the alphabet to help you.

A B C D E F G H I J K L M N O P Q R S T U V W X Y Z

BK   DM   FO   HQ   JS   (____)

- The pairs of letters are following a sequence based on their position in the alphabet.
- You have to work out what sequence they are following and then fill in the next letter pair.
- In this question both letters move forward two places in the alphabet each time. This means the next letter pair is LU.

The letters can move **Independently**

1) The letters don't always move the same number of steps or in the same direction. For example:

> FY   HU   JQ   LM   (_____)

2) The first letter moves forward 2 each time and the second letter moves back 4 each time.

The answer here is NI.

The **Sequence** can go **Over the End** of the **Alphabet**

1) Sometimes the sequence will move forwards past Z or backwards past A.
2) If this happens, just keep counting around to the other end of the alphabet.

> H   F   D   B   (_____)

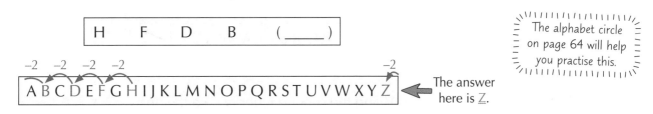

The answer here is Z.

The alphabet circle on page 64 will help you practise this.

Letter Sequences

Use the **Alphabet** to **Count Out** the **Sequence**

Find the pair of letters that continues the sequence in the best way. Use the alphabet to help you.

A B C D E F G H I J K L M N O P Q R S T U V W X Y Z

BI   FF   JC   NZ   RW   (____)

Method 1 — Look at the first three pairs

1) Find the <u>first letter</u> of the <u>first pair</u> in the <u>alphabet</u>. Then <u>count the steps</u> to the <u>first letter</u> of the <u>second pair</u>. Do the same for the <u>second</u> and <u>third</u> pairs.

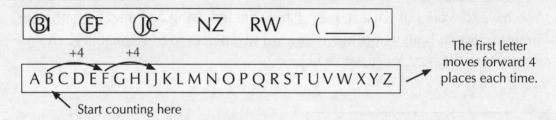

The first letter moves forward 4 places each time.

2) Look at the <u>last letter pair</u> and <u>use the sequence</u> to find the <u>first letter</u> of the <u>answer</u>.

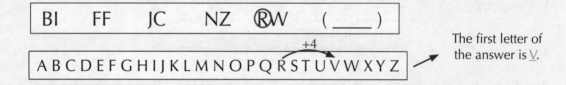

The first letter of the answer is <u>V</u>.

3) Now find the <u>second letter</u> of the <u>first pair</u> in the <u>alphabet</u>. Count the steps to the <u>second letter</u> of the <u>second pair</u>, and then to the <u>second letter</u> of the <u>third pair</u>.

The second letter moves back 3 places each time.

4) <u>Use the sequence</u> to count back from the last letter pair to find the <u>second letter</u> of the <u>answer</u>.

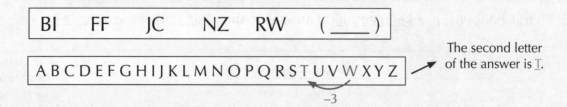

The second letter of the answer is <u>T</u>.

5) The <u>first letter</u> of the pair is <u>V</u> and the <u>second letter</u> is <u>T</u>, so the answer is <u>VT</u>.

Letter Sequences

Some Questions have more Complex Sequences

KEY EXAMPLE: BS   CQ   EP   HN   LM   (___)

Method 2 — Look at the whole sequence

1) Use this method for tricky sequences, where the gap between the pairs changes.

2) Start by looking at the first letter in the first three pairs.

B̶S̶   C̶Q̶   E̶P̶   HN   LM   (___)

+1 +2

A B C D E F G H I J K L M N O P Q R S T U V W X Y Z

> Use a pencil to note down the jump between one letter and the next — it'll stop you getting confused.

3) The jumps between the letters are different, so you need to look at all the letter pairs.

+1 +2 +3   +4   +5

A B C D E F G H I J K L M N O P Q R S T U V W X Y Z

The jump between each letter increases by 1 each time, so the next letter in the sequence will be 5 letters on from L. → The first missing letter is Q.

4) Now look at the second letter in the first three pairs.

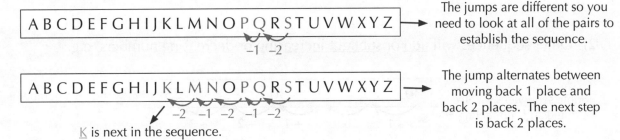

A B C D E F G H I J K L M N O P Q R S T U V W X Y Z
−1 −2

→ The jumps are different so you need to look at all of the pairs to establish the sequence.

A B C D E F G H I J K L M N O P Q R S T U V W X Y Z
−2 −1 −2 −1 −2

→ The jump alternates between moving back 1 place and back 2 places. The next step is back 2 places.

K is next in the sequence.

5) The first letter is Q and the second letter is K, so the answer is QK.

Practice Questions

Find the pair of letters that continues the sequence in the best way.
Use the alphabet at the top of the page to help you.

1) FS   KO   PK   UG   ZC   (___)

2) NE   OG   OK   NM   LQ   (___)

Look at all the pairs in more complicated sequences...

REVISION TIP

Method 1 takes less time because you only have to look at the first three pairs of letters.
If the sequence is more complicated, you'll need to use Method 2 to get the answer.

Number Sequences

These pages on Number Sequences will make this question type as easy as 1, 2, 3...

11+ Example Question

Here's an <u>example</u> question for you to look at:

 **Find the number that continues the sequence in the best way.**

48   41   34   27   (___)

- You need to work out the <u>rule</u> for the <u>number sequence</u> and use it to <u>fill in</u> the <u>missing number</u>.
- In this example the rule is to <u>subtract 7</u> each time, so the <u>answer</u> is <u>20</u>.

The Sequences follow Different Patterns

Sequences use Addition, Subtraction, Multiplication and Division

1) Simple sequences <u>add</u> or <u>subtract</u> the <u>same number</u> each time, e.g.:

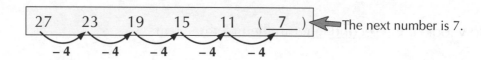

27   23   19   15   11   (__7__) ← The next number is 7.
      − 4   − 4   − 4   − 4   − 4

2) Other sequences will <u>add</u> or <u>subtract increasing</u> or <u>decreasing</u> numbers, e.g.:

Some sequences involve adding <u>and</u> subtracting.

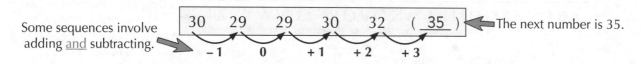

30   29   29   30   32   (__35__) ← The next number is 35.
     − 1   0   + 1   + 2   + 3

3) In some sequences the <u>previous two numbers</u> are added together to get the <u>next number</u> e.g.:

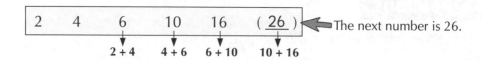

2   4   6   10   16   (__26__) ← The next number is 26.
            2 + 4   4 + 6   6 + 10 10 + 16

4) Some sequences use <u>multiplication</u> or <u>division</u>, e.g.:

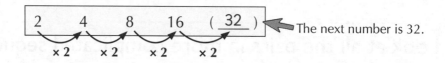

2   4   8   16   (__32__) ← The next number is 32.
   × 2   × 2   × 2   × 2

Number Sequences

Look at the **Differences** between the **Numbers**

KEY EXAMPLE: **Find the number that continues the sequence in the best way.**

11   13   17   25   41   (____)

Method 1 — Work out the difference between each number

1) Look at the sequence. Work out the <u>difference</u> between <u>each</u> of the <u>numbers</u> by <u>subtracting</u> the <u>smaller</u> one from the <u>larger</u> one.

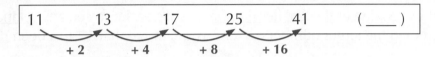

11   13   17   25   41   (____)

+ 2   + 4   + 8   + 16

2) There is a <u>pattern</u> in the <u>differences</u> between the numbers — the jump <u>doubles each time</u>.

3) Use this pattern to work out what the <u>next step</u> will be. To find the <u>next number</u> in the <u>sequence</u>, you need to <u>double 16</u> and <u>add the result</u> to the <u>last number</u>.

Now add 32 onto the last number in the sequence.

$16 \times 2 = \mathbf{32}$ ⟶ $32 + 41 = \mathbf{73}$

4) The <u>answer</u> is <u>73</u>. ⟶   11   13   17   25   41   (<u>73</u>)

KEY EXAMPLE: **Find the number that continues the sequence in the best way.**

10   25   12   21   14   17   (____)

Method 2 — Work out the difference between alternate numbers

1) Look at the sequence — if there are <u>more</u> than <u>five numbers</u>, and they <u>increase</u> and <u>decrease</u>, it's probably an <u>alternating sequence</u>.

2) Look at the <u>differences</u> between <u>alternate numbers</u>, starting from the <u>end</u> of the sequence.

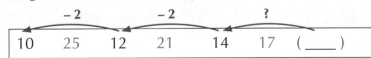

– 2   – 2   ?

10   25   12   21   14   17   (____)

> You only need to look at the sequence that leads to the answer — you can ignore the other sequence.

3) So the <u>answer</u> is <u>16</u> because if you <u>take away 2</u> from 16, it gives you 14 — the <u>previous number</u> in the sequence.

Number Sequences

Look for a **Relationship** between the **Numbers**

 **KEY EXAMPLE:** **Find the number that continues the sequence in the best way.**

96   48   24   12   6   (_____)

Method 3 — Look for multiplication or division

1) Look at the sequence to see if any of the numbers are <u>factors</u> or <u>multiples</u> of each other — sequences that contain <u>factors</u> and <u>multiples</u> usually use <u>multiplication</u> or <u>division</u>.

2) Start by looking at the <u>smaller numbers</u> — it's easier to see any <u>relationship</u> between them than the larger numbers. Here, you can see that 12 has been <u>divided by 2</u> to get <u>6</u>.

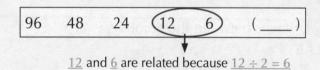

96   48   24   (12   6)   (_____)

<u>12</u> and <u>6</u> are related because $12 \div 2 = 6$

> Sequences that contain large numbers often have a rule which uses multiplication or division.

3) Once you've worked out how <u>two of the numbers</u> are <u>related</u>, you need to check whether your rule applies to the <u>other numbers in the sequence</u>. If the rule is to <u>divide by 2 each time</u> then you'd expect:

$24 \div 2 = 12$ and $48 \div 2 = 24$ and $96 \div 2 = 48$ ← These sums are <u>correct</u> so the rule <u>must be</u> to <u>divide by 2</u>.

4) Now that you know the <u>rule</u>, you need to work out the <u>missing number</u> in the <u>sequence</u>.

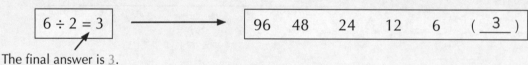

$6 \div 2 = 3$ ⟶   96   48   24   12   6   (_3_)

The final answer is <u>3</u>.

Practice Questions

Find the number that continues the sequence in the best way.

1) 52   48   43   39   (_____)

2) 15   19   25   33   (_____)

3) 37   26   19   14   (_____)

4) 243   81   27   9   (_____)

 TEST TIP

Find the balance between speed and accuracy...

You'll be able to work faster in the test if you can do most of these sums in your head, but don't worry if you have to write some of them down — it's just as important to be accurate.

Related Numbers

These questions can be really sneaky, so read these pages carefully and be prepared.

11+ Example Question

Take a look at this 11+ sample question:

 **Find the number that completes the final set of numbers in the same way as the first two sets.**

10 (12) 22   9 (8) 17   4 (____) 15

- In each set the first and third number are used in a sum to make the middle number. You need to work out how the middle numbers are made, then fill in the missing number in the third set.
- In this question, the first number is subtracted from the third number to give the middle number. So the answer is 15 − 4 = 11.

Look at the Numbers in the First Two Sets

1) If the middle number is larger than the first and third numbers the sum probably uses multiplication or addition.

   2 (8) 4   3 (15) 5   4 (_12_) 3 ➡ Multiply the first and third numbers to get the middle number.

2) If the middle number is smaller than or between the numbers either side, the sum probably uses subtraction or division.

   19 (14) 5   8 (5) 3   21 (_19_) 2 ➡ Subtract the third number from the first number to get the middle number.

3) If the numbers are factors or multiples of each other, the sum probably uses division or multiplication.

   15 (5) 3   21 (3) 7   16 (_4_) 4 ➡ Divide the first number by the third number to get the middle number.

4) Sometimes the middle number will be exactly halfway between the outer numbers.

   12 (10) 8   21 (11) 1   18 (_14_) 10 ➡ The middle number is exactly halfway between the outer numbers.

Section Four — Maths and Sequences

Related Numbers

Compare the Middle Number to the Outer Numbers

Find the number that completes the final set of numbers in the same way as the first two sets.

3 (4) 12   4 (6) 24   6 (____) 30

Method 1 — Compare the numbers

1) Look at the <u>middle number</u> in the first two sets and <u>compare</u> it to the <u>numbers on either side</u>.

> 3 (4) 12   4 (6) 24   6 (____) 30

These numbers both lie between the two numbers outside the brackets, so the rule will probably use subtraction or division.

2) Try <u>subtracting</u> and <u>dividing</u> the <u>outer numbers</u> to see which one will give the <u>middle numbers</u>. Always <u>divide</u> the <u>larger number</u> by the <u>smaller number</u> and <u>subtract</u> the <u>smaller number</u> from the <u>larger number</u>.

| 12 − 3 = 9 | ✗ | Subtracting the first number from the third number <u>doesn't give</u> the middle number, so that isn't the rule. | 24 − 4 = 20 | ✗ |

| 12 ÷ 3 = 4 | ✓ | Dividing the third number by the first number <u>gives</u> the middle number, so that <u>must be the rule</u>. | 24 ÷ 4 = 6 | ✓ |

3) The rule fits with both the <u>first</u> and <u>second number sets</u>. Now you can use it to <u>find the missing number</u> from the last set.

30 ÷ 6 = 5 ⟶ 3 (4) 12   4 (6) 24   6 (_5_) 30

The answer will always be a whole number — if you don't get one then go back and check your working.

Look at the first two sets of numbers for clues...

You can use the first two sets of numbers to help you work out whether the missing number will be bigger than, smaller than, or in-between the outer numbers in the final set. If you're doing a multiple-choice test, this might help you to quickly rule out some of the wrong answers.

Related Numbers

More **Difficult Questions** use **Rules** with **More than One Step**

KEY EXAMPLE: 11 (10) 6   14 (6) 11   19 (____) 8

Method 2 — Step by step calculation

1) Look at the <u>outer numbers</u> in each set first — the <u>first step</u> will usually use <u>both numbers</u>.

$$⑪(10)⑥ \quad ⑭(6)⑪ \quad\quad 19 (\underline{\quad}) 8$$

2) The <u>outer numbers</u> aren't <u>factors</u> or <u>multiples</u> of each other, so the sum probably doesn't use <u>multiplication</u> or <u>division</u> first. It probably uses <u>addition</u> or <u>subtraction</u> — you'll need to try both.

There's more on factors and multiples on page 63.

3) <u>Add</u> the <u>outer numbers</u> in each set and see if the <u>answer</u> is <u>linked</u> to the <u>middle number</u>.

Compare the answers with the middle number from each set.

| $11 + 6 = \mathbf{17}$ | and | $14 + 11 = \mathbf{25}$ |

10 and **17** → No obvious connections. ← **6** and **25**

4) <u>Adding</u> the <u>outer numbers</u> doesn't reveal any <u>obvious link</u> to the <u>middle number</u>, so try <u>subtracting</u> the <u>outer numbers</u>.

Compare the answers with the middle number from each set.

| $11 - 6 = \mathbf{5}$ | and | $14 - 11 = \mathbf{3}$ |

10 and **5**   **6** and **3**

For both sets you can multiply the answer by 2 to get the middle number.

5) So the rule is to <u>subtract the third number from the first</u> and then <u>double the answer</u>. Now use the <u>rule</u> with the <u>numbers</u> from the <u>third set</u> to get the <u>missing number</u>:

$$19 - 8 = 11 \quad\longrightarrow\quad 11 \times 2 = 22 \quad\longleftarrow \text{ The final answer is } \underline{22}.$$

Practice Questions

Find the number that completes the final set of numbers in the same way as the first two sets.

1) 17 (21) 4   9 (24) 15   31 (____) 7

2) 9 (17) 2   4 (23) 6   8 (____) 4

3) 5 (6) 15   7 (10) 35   4 (____) 16

4) 15 (22) 29   8 (12) 16   17 (____) 27

TEST TIP

Try to narrow down your options...

Before you try to add, subtract, multiply or divide the sets of outer numbers, think about the numbers in the first two sets. Work out which calculations are most likely to have been used to get the middle numbers. Then, have a go at using these calculations on the third set.

Letter-Coded Sums

Letter-Coded Sums are just sums where the numbers have been swapped for letters.

11+ Example Question

Here's an <u>example</u> of the kind of question you might get in the test:

Each letter stands for a number. Work out the answer to the sum as a letter.

$A = 2$ $B = 3$ $C = 5$ $D = 9$ $E = 11$ $D \div B + A = ($ _____ $)$

- <u>Use the code</u> to work out the <u>answer to the sum</u> using <u>numbers</u>.
  Then change the <u>answer</u> into a <u>letter</u>.
- The <u>answer is C</u> because $9 \div 3 + 2 = 5$, and <u>C is the code for 5</u>.

Work through the sum **Step by Step**

1) <u>Letter-Coded Sums</u> often have <u>calculations</u> with <u>2 or 3 steps</u>.

2) When you're working through a calculation you need to work out the <u>answer to each step</u> and then <u>use that answer</u> in the <u>next step</u> of the sum. For example:

$A = 2$ $B = 3$ $C = 6$ $D = 16$ $E = 18$ $C \times B - A = ($ _____ $)$

Start by working out the answer to the <u>first part</u> of the <u>calculation</u>.

$C \times B$ ⇒ 6×3 ⇒ 18

Then, do the same for the <u>second step</u> in the calculation.

$18 - A$ ⇒ $18 - 2$ ⇒ 16

Now <u>convert</u> 16 to a <u>letter</u>.

$16 = D$

D is the <u>code</u> for 16, so D is the <u>answer</u> you write down.

Save time with times tables...

REVISION TIP

Letter-Coded Sums questions involve multiplication and division, so this is another type of question where knowing your times tables is going to save you lots of time in the test.

Letter-Coded Sums

Change the **Letters** into **Numbers**

Each letter stands for a number. Work out the answer to the sum as a letter.

A = 3   B = 4   C = 8   D = 12   E = 18   D × B ÷ C + D = (____)

Method — Decode the sum

1) Look at the sum. Use the code in the question to change each letter into a number.

D × B ÷ C + D = (____)   →   12 × 4 ÷ 8 + 12 = (____)

↑ ↑ ↑ ↑
12 4 8 12

2) Work through the sum step by step in order.

12 × 4 = 48   →   48 ÷ 8 = 6   →   6 + 12 = 18

3) You need to write your answer as a letter, not a number.
Look back at the code in the question to see which letter is used for 18.

A = 3   B = 4   C = 8   D = 12   (E = 18)

If the number you get doesn't match any of the letters, go back and check your working.

4) 18 is equal to E in the code, so the answer is E.

Practice Questions

Each letter stands for a number. Work out the answer to the sum as a letter.

1) A = 2   B = 4   C = 7   D = 21   E = 28   C × B = (____)

2) A = 3   B = 7   C = 11   D = 14   E = 19   C × A − D = (____)

3) A = 3   B = 6   C = 9   D = 15   E = 45   E ÷ C × A = (____)

4) A = 4   B = 12   C = 17   D = 21   E = 27   B × A − C − E = (____)

Keep a note of your working as you go...

Even if you can work out the sums in your head, it's a good idea to write down the answer you get at each step of the calculation — it'll stop you getting confused if you lose your place in the sum.

Practice Questions

Now you've worked your way through the Maths and Sequences section, have a go at these practice questions. They'll give you a chance to put your new skills into action.

Complete the Sum

> Find the missing number to complete each sum.
> Write your answer on the line. Look at this example:
>
> **Example:** $20 \div 4 = 3 + ($ _2_ $)$

1. $49 \div 7 = 1 + ($ _____ $)$

2. $9 + 3 = 36 \div ($ _____ $)$

3. $25 - 7 = 2 \times ($ _____ $)$

4. $14 \div 7 = 19 - ($ _____ $)$

5. $2 \times 11 + 14 = 39 - ($ _____ $)$

6. $21 \div 7 + 4 = 17 - ($ _____ $)$

7. $4 \times 8 + 14 = 45 + ($ _____ $)$

8. $90 \div 9 + 13 = 20 + ($ _____ $)$

9. $49 - 10 + 13 = 40 + ($ _____ $)$

10. $3 + 29 - 10 = 2 \times ($ _____ $)$

11. $42 \div 6 + 31 = 14 + ($ _____ $)$

12. $4 \times 9 + 7 = 31 + ($ _____ $)$

Practice Questions

Letter Sequences

Find the pair of letters that continues each sequence in the best way. Use the alphabet to help you:

A B C D E F G H I J K L M N O P Q R S T U V W X Y Z

Look at this example:

Example: BC   DE   FG   HI   JK   (<u>LM</u>)

13. KU   JV   KT   JU   KS   (_____)

14. AV   ZA   XZ   WE   UD   (_____)

15. TT   WP   VM   YI   XF   (_____)

16. DP   FT   HW   JY   LZ   (_____)

17. SL   NQ   IU   DX   YZ   (_____)

18. CX   HY   IB   NC   OF   (_____)

19. AK   ZO   ZS   AW   CA   (_____)

20. WN   AJ   CG   GE   ID   (_____)

21. ZW   AZ   AV   ZY   XU   (_____)

22. BV   GX   LY   QY   VX   (_____)

23. HD   GC   FA   EX   DT   (_____)

24. ZC   YA   CZ   BZ   FA   (_____)

Practice Questions

Number Sequences

Find the number that continues each sequence in the best way.
Write your answer on the line. Look at this example:

Example: 1   3   5   7   9   (__11__)

25. 49   41   33   25   17   (_____)

26. 32   16   8   4   2   (_____)

27. 7   12   16   19   21   (_____)

28. 8   19   11   12   14   5   (_____)

29. 29   22   30   32   31   (_____)

30. 15   21   26   30   33   (_____)

31. 4   5   8   13   20   (_____)

32. 42   40   39   39   40   (_____)

33. 5   7   11   17   25   (_____)

34. 25   11   18   15   11   19   (_____)

35. 3   59   6   54   12   49   (_____)

36. 120   120   60   20   5   (_____)

Practice Questions

Related Numbers

Find the number that completes the final set of numbers in the same way as the first two sets. Write your answer on the line. Look at this example:

Example: 1 (3) 2   3 (7) 4   10 (**12**) 2

37. 18 (3) 3   30 (5) 3   20 (_____) 10

38. 1 (4) 7   8 (7) 3   6 (_____) 7

39. 5 (6) 3   9 (20) 5   7 (_____) 6

40. 9 (7) 7   10 (14) 1   16 (_____) 9

41. 4 (10) 5   4 (18) 9   6 (_____) 3

42. 10 (63) 7   8 (28) 4   8 (_____) 5

43. 6 (15) 2   80 (40) 10   64 (_____) 8

44. 4 (12) 5   2 (14) 11   3 (_____) 4

45. 9 (30) 6   8 (24) 4   4 (_____) 9

46. 2 (2) 10   10 (3) 8   8 (_____) 16

47. 5 (4) 5   10 (5) 9   12 (_____) 5

48. 6 (18) 4   3 (9) 4   2 (_____) 7

Practice Questions

Letter-Coded Sums

Each letter stands for a number. Work out the answer to each sum as a letter.
Write your answer on the line. Look at this example:

Example: A = 1 B = 2 C = 6 D = 8 E = 12   B × C = (__E__)

49. A = 1   B = 4   C = 9   D = 15 E = 21   E − C + B − D = (_____)

50. A = 2   B = 4   C = 8   D = 13 E = 24   E ÷ B + A = (_____)

51. A = 2   B = 5   C = 6   D = 8   E = 17   B + C − A + D = (_____)

52. A = 1   B = 5   C = 6   D = 8   E = 10   E ÷ B × A + C = (_____)

53. A = 2   B = 3   C = 9   D = 11 E = 29   C × A + D = (_____)

54. A = 3   B = 6   C = 9   D = 13 E = 14   B × A + C − D = (_____)

55. A = 3   B = 6   C = 8   D = 9   E = 21   E ÷ A + C − D = (_____)

56. A = 3   B = 8   C = 10 D = 13 E = 25   A × C + B − D = (_____)

57. A = 1   B = 2   C = 8   D = 10 E = 13   D × B + A − E = (_____)

58. A = 9   B = 11 C = 14 D = 21 E = 28   B − A × D − E = (_____)

59. A = 5   B = 9   C = 13 D = 15 E = 27   E ÷ B + D − C = (_____)

60. A = 1   B = 2   C = 3   D = 14 E = 29   D × B + C − E = (_____)

Preparing for the Test

Verbal Reasoning tests more than your vocab and maths skills — you also need to think logically.

You need to be **Accurate** to do well in **Coding Questions**

Coding questions test a range of skills:
1) Using the alphabet and counting accurately along it.
2) Spotting patterns and working out the next step.
3) Using logic to solve problems quickly.

> **Doing lots of practice will make Coding Questions easier**

1) Do number and alphabet puzzles in puzzle books or on the internet.
2) Practise counting along the alphabet — use the alphabet circle on page 64 to help you practise counting backwards from A or forwards from Z.
3) Practise spotting letter pairs that are an equal distance from the centre of the alphabet. For example, the letters E and V are five letters in from each end of the alphabet, or nine letters out from the centre of the alphabet.

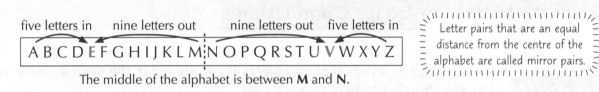

five letters in   nine letters out   nine letters out   five letters in

A B C D E F G H I J K L M | N O P Q R S T U V W X Y Z

The middle of the alphabet is between **M** and **N**.

Letter pairs that are an equal distance from the centre of the alphabet are called mirror pairs.

Logic Questions use lots of different skills

To do well in logic questions you need to be able to:
1) Read and understand information and pay attention to details.
2) Pick out key pieces of information to solve a problem, and ignore the bits that are irrelevant.
3) Do simple maths quickly.

> **You can Practise Logical Thinking in different ways**

1) Buy a puzzle magazine — these often have puzzles just like Solve the Riddle (p.93-95) and Word Grids (p.96-97). There are puzzles like this on the internet too.
2) Play games like 'Cluedo' or 'Guess Who?' to test your powers of deduction and logic.
3) Play 'Twenty Questions' with a friend — it'll help you practise dealing with information.
4) Practise doing sums which use addition and subtraction — doing other Verbal Reasoning questions that use maths will help with this too.
5) Practise putting information into a table — you could ask your friends what pets they have or what shoe size they are and put their answers in a table.

Letter Connections

Letter Connections is another question type that uses the alphabet — you just can't escape it.

11+ **Example** Question

Here's an <u>example</u> of the sort of question you might get in the <u>test</u>:

> **KEY EXAMPLE:**
>
> **Find the pair of letters that completes the sentence in the most sensible way. Use the alphabet to help you.**
>
> A B C D E F G H I J K L M N O P Q R S T U V W X Y Z
>
> **SF** is to **PH** as **FB** is to (____).

- There is a <u>connection</u> between the first <u>two letter pairs</u> — you need to work out what this <u>connection</u> is and then <u>apply</u> it to the second pair to find the <u>missing letters</u>.
- The answer is <u>CD</u> — the <u>first letters</u> are connected by moving <u>back three places</u>. The <u>second letters</u> are connected by moving <u>forward two places</u>.

Count the **Letters** to find the **Connection**

> **KEY EXAMPLE:**
>
> **Find the pair of letters that completes the sentence in the most sensible way. Use the alphabet to help you.**
>
> A B C D E F G H I J K L M N O P Q R S T U V W X Y Z
>
> **GD** is to **JE** as **SB** is to (____).

Method 1 — Count along the alphabet

1) Check to make sure that there aren't any <u>mirror pairs</u> — there aren't any in this example.

2) Next you need to count along the alphabet to see how the <u>first letter</u> in the <u>first pair</u> is connected to the <u>first letter</u> in the <u>second pair</u>.

> *It doesn't matter how the letters within each pair are connected.*

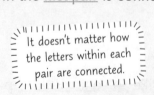

GD is to **JE** as **SB** is to (V)

These letters are connected by moving forward 3 places.

Use the connection between the first letters to find the first missing letter.

3) The <u>second letter</u> in the <u>first pair</u> is connected to the <u>second letter</u> in the <u>second pair</u>.

These letters are connected by moving forward 1 place.

Use the connection between the second letters to find the second missing letter.

> *The letters don't have to move in the same way — they can be completely independent.*

GD is to **JE** as **SB** is to (VC)

Letter Connections

Check for **Mirror Pairs First**

KEY EXAMPLE:

Find the pair of letters that completes the sentence in the most sensible way. Use the alphabet to help you.

A B C D E F G H I J K L M N O P Q R S T U V W X Y Z

ZU is to **FA** as **XS** is to (_____).

Method 2 — Use mirror pairs

1) Check the question for <u>mirror pairs</u>. At first glance it may not look like there are any, but on <u>closer inspection</u>...

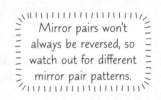
Mirror pairs won't always be reversed, so watch out for different mirror pair patterns.

AZ is a mirror pair, but it's been reversed.

ZU is to **FA** as **XS** is to (_____).

FU is also a mirror pair and it's been reversed too.

2) The <u>answer</u> will use mirror pairs in the <u>same way</u> as the <u>first pair</u> of letters. The letters in the second pair are **XS**, so find their <u>mirror pairs</u>.

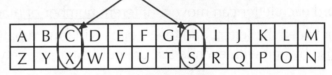

| A | B | C | D | E | F | G | H | I | J | K | L | M |
| Z | Y | X | W | V | U | T | S | R | Q | P | O | N |

3) The matching letters are '<u>C</u>' and '<u>H</u>'. Now you have to put these letters in the <u>same order</u> as the first pair of letters.

4) So the <u>answer</u> is: ➔ **ZU** is to **FA** as **XS** is to (<u>HC</u>).

Practice Questions

Find the pair of letters that completes the sentence in the most sensible way.

1)   **DW** is to **FU** as **IR** is to (_____).

2)   **PF** is to **TB** as **VC** is to (_____).

3)   **NG** is to **ON** as **SE** is to (_____).

4)   **BE** is to **YV** as **HK** is to (_____).

REVISION TIP

You need to know how to spot mirror pairs...

If you treat a mirror pair like a standard pair of letters, you'll get the wrong answer. Get to know the mirror pairs in the grid above so that you can spot them more easily in the test.

Letter-Word Codes

Accurate counting is the key to answering Letter-Word Codes questions.

11+ Example Question

Here's an <u>example</u> of the sort of question you might get in the real thing:

 **KEY EXAMPLE:** **Each question uses a different code.**
Use the alphabet to help you work out the answer.

A B C D E F G H I J K L M N O P Q R S T U V W X Y Z

If the code for **TIN** is **VKP**, what is the code for **MOP?** _____

- You need to <u>work out</u> how to get from the <u>first word</u> to its <u>code</u>, then use the <u>rule</u> to find the <u>code</u> for the <u>second word</u>.
- To find the <u>code</u>, each letter moves <u>2 places</u> along the <u>alphabet</u>, so the answer is <u>OQR</u>.

The **Letters** can move in **Patterns**

1) Within a word each <u>letter</u> can move a <u>different number of places</u> and in a <u>different direction</u>.
2) The <u>jumps</u> between the <u>letters</u> and their <u>codes</u> will form a <u>pattern</u>, e.g. the <u>jumps</u> could <u>increase by one</u> with each letter, or could <u>alternate</u> between <u>two numbers</u>.

Continuing the connection

If the code for **BACK** is **CDDN**, what is the code for **FRUIT?** _____

1) The second <u>word code</u> can be <u>longer</u> than the first one. In the example above, **BACK** is <u>four</u> letters long whereas **FRUIT** is <u>five</u> letters long.

2) To get from the <u>word to the code</u> the letters move <u>forward one place</u>, then <u>forward three places</u> alternately.

B	— +1 →	C
A	— +3 →	D
C	— +1 →	D
K	— +3 →	N

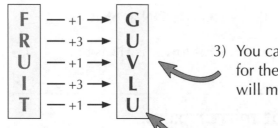

3) You can <u>assume the pattern continues</u> for the extra letter, so the <u>fifth letter</u> will move <u>forward one place</u>.

The answer is <u>GUVLU</u>.

Section Five — Logic and Coding

Letter-Word Codes

If you're looking for a **Word**, count from the **Code** to the **Word**

Each question uses a different code.
Use the alphabet to help you work out the answer.

A B C D E F G H I J K L M N O P Q R S T U V W X Y Z

If the code for **TUBE** is **SQAA**, what is **AQMG** the code for? _____

Method 1 — Count along the alphabet line

1) Look at the question and check for <u>mirror pairs</u> — there aren't any in this example.

2) Work out if you're looking for a <u>word</u> or a <u>code</u> — here, you've been given a <u>code</u> (AQMG), so you're looking for a <u>word</u>.

> If you're looking for a code, you need to work out how to get from the word to the code in the first pair.

3) When you're looking for a <u>word</u>, look at how you get from the <u>code</u> to the <u>word</u> in the <u>first pair</u> of words.

Draw an arrow to <u>remind</u> you <u>which way</u> you're <u>solving</u> the question. → If the code for **TUBE** is **SQAA**

4) <u>Count</u> from each letter of the <u>code</u> to the <u>matching</u> letter of the <u>word</u>.

```
      +1                          +1
A B C D E F G H I J K L M N O P Q R S T U V W X Y Z
    +4                          +4
```

S	— +1 →	T
Q	— +4 →	U
A	— +1 →	B
A	— +4 →	E

To get from the code to the word the letters move in the pattern
+1, +4, +1, +4.

5) Once you <u>know</u> the <u>connection</u> between the <u>word</u> and the <u>code</u>, you can find the <u>missing word</u>.

A	— +1 →	B
Q	— +4 →	U
M	— +1 →	N
G	— +4 →	K

To get from the code to the word move the letters in the same pattern.

6) The <u>missing word</u> is <u>BUNK</u>.

Don't work out more than you need to...

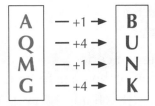

If you're sitting a multiple-choice test, you might only need to work out the first few letters to find the answer. If you have time at the end of the test, go back and check your answer.

Letter-Word Codes

Some questions use **Mirror Codes**

KEY EXAMPLE: If the code for **STORM** is **HGLIN**, what is **GLDVI** the code for? _____

Method 2 — Check for mirror pairs

1) Mirror pairs can also pop up in Letter-Word Code questions. Here's a reminder of the mirror pairs:

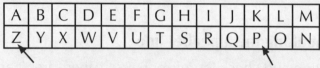

> In questions that use mirror pairs the same letters always code for each other.

Each column is a mirror pair, e.g. A and Z or K and P.

2) Look at the first letters of the word and the code you are given to see if they are a mirror pair.

$S \rightarrow H$, S and H are a mirror pair.

3) The first letters could be a mirror pair by chance — look at the next two pairs to double check.

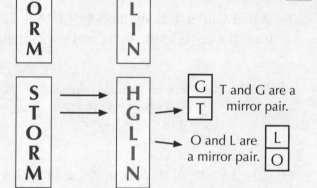

T and G are a mirror pair.

O and L are a mirror pair.

4) Now that you're sure it's a mirror code, use mirror pairs to find the missing word.

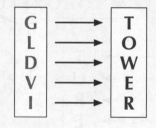

5) The answer is TOWER.

> If you're looking for a word and your answer doesn't make sense, double check your working.

Practice Questions

Each question uses a different code.
Use the alphabet at the top of the page to help you to answer each question.

1) If the code for **BED** is **GJI**, what is the code for **FIG**? _____

2) If the code for **SNOOP** is **VKRLS**, what is **OLBXO** the code for? _____

3) If the code for **HUNT** is **JXRY**, what is the code for **BRING**? _____

Using a mirror pair grid will help to make everything clear...

Write out a mirror pair grid on a spare piece of paper to help you quickly check for mirror pairs.

Number-Word Codes

These questions come up a lot, so make sure you know how to answer them.

11+ Example Question

Here's an example question for you to take a look at:

The number codes for three of these four words are listed in a random order. Work out the code to answer the question.

WEAK   TAKE   PEAT   KEPT

3265   5612   4261

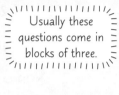

Usually these questions come in blocks of three.

Find the code for the word **WEPT**. _____

- Use the number codes you're given to work out which number stands for which letter.
- Then you use the code to answer the question — it might be to find a code or a word.

Look for **Patterns** in the **Numbers**

Find the code for the word **WEPT**. _____

Method 1 — Look at the numbers first

1) Look at the numbers to see if there are any similar patterns.

    ⟨3265⟩   5612   ⟨4261⟩ ← Both these codes have '26' in the middle.

2) Find the two words that have same two letters in the middle.

    ⟨WEAK⟩   TAKE   ⟨PEAT⟩   KEPT → **WEAK** and **PEAT** are the only two words that have the same two letters in the middle, so 2 = E and 6 = A.

3) Look at the third number, 5612.

    5 6 1 2   →   You know that 2 = E and 6 = A, so you can write these letters below the code. The only word which fits this code is **TAKE**.   →   5 6 1 2
    ? A ? E   T A K E

4) Go back to the first two codes and fill in any other letters that you can. You know that 5 = T and 1 = K, so 3265 must code for **PEAT**, and 4261 must code for **WEAK**.
    → 3 2 6 5   4 2 6 1
         P E A T   W E A K

5) Now you know the number for each letter, you can work out the code for **WEPT**, 4235.

Number-Word Codes

Compare the Letters in all the words

BELT   DUEL   LUTE   TUBE
6415   1526   3452

Find the word that has the number code **1245**. _____

Method 2 — Look for letters in the same position in different words

1) Look at the number codes to see if there are any patterns.

2) None of the number codes end with the same number, so the code for LUTE or TUBE must be missing. Look for other letters that are in the same position in different words.

> BELT   D(U)EL   L(U)TE   T(U)BE   →   Three of the words have U as a second letter.

3) Look at the number codes. 4 is the second number in two of them, so 4 must be the code for U.

4) BELT is the only word that doesn't have U as its second letter, so the number code that has a different second number must be the code for BELT.

> 6 4 1 5   1 5 2 6   3 4 5 2
> ? U ? ?   B E L T   ? U ? ?

5) Now you can use the code for BELT to crack the other codes and answer the question.

> The code that starts with 6 must be the word starting with T. → 6 4 1 5   T U B E
>
> The last code left ends in 2, so this must be the code for the only word ending in L. → 3 4 5 2   D U E L

6) So, the answer is BLUE. → 1 2 4 5   B L U E

Practice Questions

LONE   RENT   NOTE   TOOL
1432   6412   5213

1) Find the code for the word **TOOL**. _____

2) Find the code for the word **TORN**. _____

3) Find the word that has the number code **5466**. _____

You can use either of these methods to get the answer...

Try practising each of the methods for this question type and see which one works best for you.

Explore the Facts

This is the first of the logic questions — you'll really need your thinking cap on for these.

 **11+ Example** Question

Take a look at this 11+ sample question:

> **EXAMPLE:** **Read the information carefully, then use it to answer the question that follows.**
>
> Gita, Heung, Joseph, Penny and Mark go to an outdoor activity centre. Gita, Penny and Heung go rafting. Joseph and Heung go caving. Everyone except Gita goes rock climbing. Only Mark goes on the zipwire. Penny does 3 activities.
>
> Who does the **fewest** activities? _____

- You need to read all the information you are given and then use it to answer the question.
- The answer is Gita — when you work through the statements you see that:

    1) Penny does three activities (including rafting and rock climbing).
    2) Heung does three activities (rafting, caving and rock climbing).
    3) Joseph does two activities (caving and rock climbing).
    4) Mark also does two activities (rock climbing and zipwire).
    5) Gita only does one activity (rafting).

Read the **Statements** carefully

1) The wording of some phrases in these questions might catch you out.
2) You can't always just count who does what — look out for phrases like these:

| 'All the children...' | 'All the boys...' | 'Everyone except...' |

| 'Kieran did not...' | 'The only one who...' |

3) The question could ask you to look for the person who does the most or the fewest things. Make sure you read each sentence carefully so you know what each person is or isn't doing.

 ## Slow and steady wins the race...

These types of questions are often full of tricky wording to make sure you're reading the passage carefully. Read the text more than once to make sure you understand it all.

Explore the Facts

Write the Information down

EXAMPLE: Molly, Ceana, Matt, Dee and Steven are talking about their favourite animals. Molly and Matt like pigs. Matt likes cows. Ceana and Steven like horses. Everyone except Dee likes cows. Dee and Steven like sheep and goats.

Who likes the **most** animals? _____

Method — Make a table

1) Read the question carefully — you need to work out who likes the most animals.

2) Cross out any repeated information so you don't count it twice.

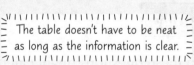

~~Matt likes cows.~~ Ceana and Steven like horses. Everyone except Dee likes cows.

3) Read the statements and then put the information into a quick tally chart. Just write the initials — it's quicker than writing whole names.

If two names have the same initial write the second letter too.

4) Read through each sentence and put a mark next to each initial for the animals they like.

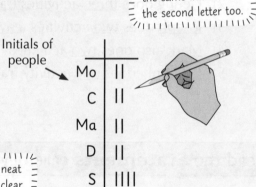

Initials of people →

Mo	II
C	II
Ma	II
D	II
S	IIII

5) Read off the table to answer the question. You're looking for the person who likes the most animals — so that's the person who has the most marks next to their initial.

6) The answer is Steven.

The table doesn't have to be neat as long as the information is clear.

Practice Question

Read the information carefully, then use it to answer the question that follows.

Glen, Ali, Kim, Marta and Luca are looking out of the windows of the school bus. Glen and Marta see a pedestrian and a cat. Kim, Ali and Luca see a yellow car. Marta and Ali see a tractor. Everyone except Kim sees a cyclist.

Who sees the **most** different things? _____

 TEST TIP

Use your time wisely to get the most marks...

Remember these questions are only worth one mark each — in the test, make a note of where in the paper they are, then come back to them at the end if you have time.

Solve the Riddle

There's lots of information in these questions, so make sure you read each sentence carefully.

11+ Example Question

You'll be asked questions like this one in the test:

Read the information carefully, then use it to answer the question that follows.

Aileen, Pascal, Jen, Marie and Louis are talking about their cousins. Marie has 3 cousins. Jen has more cousins than Louis. Aileen has one fewer cousin than Marie. Louis has twice the number of cousins Aileen has. Pascal has no aunts or uncles.

If these statements are true, only one of the sentences below **cannot** be true. Which one?

- **A** Aileen is the oldest of her cousins.
- **B** Jen has 5 cousins.
- **C** Pascal has the fewest cousins.
- **D** Louis has 6 cousins.
- **E** Aileen is Jen's cousin.

- Only one option is definitely not true. You need to use the information to work out which one.
- The answer is D:

  1) Louis has twice the number of cousins Aileen has.
  2) Aileen has one fewer cousin than Marie.
  3) Marie has 3 cousins, so Aileen has 2.
  4) This means that Louis must have 4 cousins, not 6.

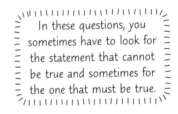

In these questions, you sometimes have to look for the statement that cannot be true and sometimes for the one that must be true.

There are different **Types** of **Solve the Riddle** questions

1) Solve the Riddle questions will often expect you to put information in order. You might have to order things by time or date, or from oldest to youngest, fastest to slowest, etc.

2) You might not be able to put all the information in order, but you'll always be given enough to answer the question.

3) For some questions you have to use simple maths, e.g. working out people's scores in a game.

These questions are also only worth 1 mark — skip them and come back to them at the end if you have time.

When you know, you know...

You can narrow down the possible answers by discounting any options that may or may not be true. For example, in the example question above, Aileen could be Jen's cousin, but you don't know for sure. If the text doesn't confirm whether something is true or not true, then it can't be the answer.

Solve the Riddle

Rule out the **Options** that are definitely **Wrong**

 **KEY EXAMPLE:**

Read the information carefully, then use it to answer the question that follows.

Donald, Ola, Sascha, Sarah and Ravi are playing a word game.
Donald scores 96. Ravi wins. Sascha scores 8 more than Donald.
Ola scores 30 less than Sascha. Sarah scores 78.

If these statements are true, only one of the sentences below **must** be true.
Which one?

    A   Ravi scores 110.
    B   Ola comes last.
    C   Sascha scores less than Sarah.
    D   Sarah scores 3 more than Ola.
    E   Ola has never played before.

Method 1 — Look for definite facts first

1) Look at the 5 options. The correct answer will be directly related to the information in the question — scan the options to see if any are unrelated.

> ~~E   Ola has never played before.~~ ←   You aren't told who has played before so you can ignore this one.

2) To decide between the other options you need to do some maths to work out what each person scored. First, find any statements that tell you exactly what someone scored.

> Donald scores 96.   Sarah scores 78.

3) Look at the other statements and use the information to work out each person's score.

> Sascha scores 8 more than Donald. → Donald scores 96, so Sascha scores 96 + 8 = 104.

> Ola scores 30 less than Sascha. → Sascha scores 104, so Ola scores 104 – 30 = 74.

> Ravi wins. → This means Ravi scores more than everyone else, so he must score more than 104.

4) Now you know everyone's scores, write them as a list and then use the information to choose which statement is true.

> Ignore any options that could be true — you're looking for the one that must be true.

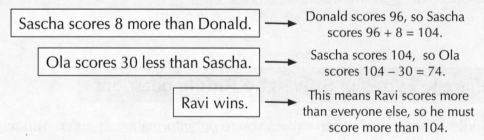

Write as much of each person's name as you need to — it'll stop you getting mixed up.

R — 104+
Sas — 104
D — 96
Sar — 78
O — 74

→

A   Ravi scores 110. **?**
B   Ola comes last. ✓
C   Sascha scores less than Sarah. ✗
D   Sarah scores 3 more than Ola. ✗
~~**E**   Ola has never played before.~~

5) The only statement that must be true is B.

Solve the Riddle

Think about how the **Statements Fit Together**

KEY EXAMPLE:

Read the information carefully, then use it to answer the question that follows.

Caitlyn, Stuart, Luke, Mandy and Polly are going to the cinema.
Luke arrives before Caitlyn and Mandy. Polly arrives second.
The third person to arrive is a boy.

If these statements are true, only one of the sentences below **cannot** be true.
Which one?

    A Stuart arrives first.
    B Polly arrives before Luke.
    C Mandy arrives before Polly.
    D Caitlyn and Mandy arrive together.
    E Caitlyn arrives after Polly.

Method 2 — Look at each statement one by one

1) Read the statements. You need to work out the order in which everyone arrived.

2) You know Polly is second. Use the other statements to work out when the others arrive.

    | The third person to arrive is a boy. | → Only Luke or Stuart can arrive third.

    | Luke arrives before Caitlyn and Mandy. | → Luke must arrive first or third, so Caitlyn and Mandy must arrive fourth and fifth. If the two girls arrive fourth and fifth, Stuart can only arrive first or third.

3) Scribble down the order they could arrive. ⟶

    1st — L / S
    2nd — P
    3rd — L / S
    4th — C / M
    5th — C / M

4) Use your list to choose the correct answer.
    Here you're looking for the only one that cannot be true.

5) You know Mandy must arrive after Polly, so the answer is C.

Practice Question

Read the information carefully, then use it to answer the question that follows.
Ellie, Mike, Nathan, Zach and Li are competing in a sack race on sports day.
Mike comes fourth. Zach isn't last. Ellie doesn't win. Li beats Zach. Nathan beats Li.

If these statements are true, only one of the sentences below **cannot** be true. Which one?

  A Ellie comes last.   **C** Ellie falls over.   **E** Li comes third.
  B Zach beats Mike.   **D** Nathan wins.

Don't rush when you're reading the questions...

Take a moment to make sure you understand exactly what a question is asking before
you answer. If you rush, you could misunderstand the question and answer it incorrectly.

Word Grids

These are a bit like doing a jigsaw puzzle — but with words instead of pictures.

11+ Example Question

Take a look at this 11+ sample question:

**EXAMPLE:** **Use the words to fill in the blanks in the word grid. You must use all the words. One letter has been filled in for you.**

puffin, coward, picnic, nagged, fellow

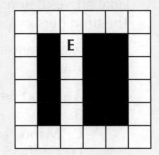

Method 1 — Use the letter you're given

1) Look at the letter in the grid. Count along the grid to find out what position in the word it is. Here E is the second letter in the word.

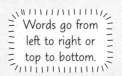
Words go from left to right or top to bottom.

2) Look at the possible words to see which one has E as its second letter.

puffin, coward, picnic, nagged, fellow → 'fellow' is the only word that fits.

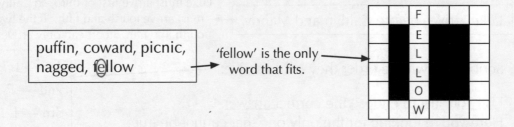

3) Now you have clues for two of the other words in the grid — one has W as the third letter and one has F as the third letter.

'puffin' has F as its third letter, so it must go along the top. ← puffin, coward, picnic, nagged, fellow → 'coward' has W as its third letter, so it must go along the bottom.

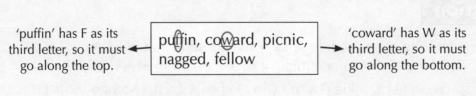

4) Then use the words you've got left to fill in the gaps.

Word Grids

Think Ahead to solve **Harder** questions

 **EXAMPLE:**
Use the words to fill in the blanks in the word grid. You must use all the words. One letter has been filled in for you.

digest, frothy, frying,
agency, govern, armour

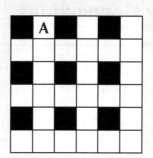

Method 2 — Look for shared letters

1) <u>Look</u> at the letter in the grid — you need a <u>word</u> that <u>starts with A</u>.

digest, frothy, frying,
ⓐgency, govern, ⓐrmour → Two words start with A.

A is the first letter in a word.

2) The word shares its <u>last letter</u> with the <u>second letter</u> of the <u>bottom word</u>. <u>Look</u> at the last letters of 'agency' and 'armour' to see if they are <u>second letters</u> of <u>other words</u>.

digest, frothy, frying,
agencⓨ govern, armouⓡ → The last letters are Y and R. Y isn't the second letter of any word, but R is, so the first word must be 'armour'. → digest, fⓡothy, fⓡying, agency, govern, armour

3) Either '<u>frying</u>' or '<u>frothy</u>' must go along the <u>bottom</u> — the <u>last letter</u> along the <u>bottom</u> is <u>shared</u> with the <u>word</u> down the <u>right hand side</u>.

digest, frothⓨ frying,
agencⓨ govern, ~~armour~~ → No words except 'frying' end in g, but 'frothy' shares its last letter with 'agency'.

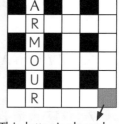

This letter is shared.

4) '<u>frothy</u>' must go along the <u>bottom</u> and '<u>agency</u>' must go down the <u>right hand side</u>.

5) Now you've got a <u>few words</u> in the <u>grid</u> you can <u>fit</u> the <u>rest of the words in</u>.

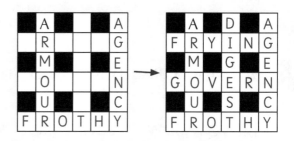

Getting started is the tricky part...

The first few words are the hardest in Word Grids because it's not always immediately obvious which word goes where. But once you've worked out a few, the rest will fall into place more easily.

Practice Questions

Have a go at these Logic and Coding practice questions to test what you've learnt in this section.

Letter Connections

Mark the pair of letters that completes each sentence in the most sensible way. Use the alphabet to help you:

A B C D E F G H I J K L M N O P Q R S T U V W X Y Z

Look at this example:

Example: **DC** is to **FE** as **MK** is to (OC <u>OM</u> FC PM NM)

1. **AG** is to **EK** as **BS** is to   (FW   IW   GZ   FY   FZ)

2. **CG** is to **WA** as **UX** is to   (OR   OS   OO   LO   LS)

3. **JV** is to **DX** as **HW** is to   (EB   YY   BW   BV   BY)

4. **DU** is to **WF** as **FY** is to   (UA   VB   UZ   UB   TA)

5. **XF** is to **UI** as **JA** is to   (GE   DB   GA   JB   GD)

6. **ZV** is to **AE** as **QW** is to   (HZ   JB   LD   KD   JD)

7. **GZ** is to **HX** as **UE** is to   (VB   VD   UD   VC   WB)

8. **XO** is to **CL** as **TN** is to   (IM   GO   HM   GM   IO)

9. **WP** is to **DK** as **XY** is to   (CD   AZ   CB   CC   AC)

10. **VQ** is to **PW** as **XC** is to   (RG   RK   UG   OH   RI)

11. **IK** is to **GO** as **WF** is to   (TH   SL   UJ   TJ   UM)

12. **HL** is to **SO** as **AM** is to   (XO   ZN   ZO   YN   ZH)

Practice Questions

Letter-Word Codes

Each question uses a different code. Use the alphabet to help you work out the answer to each question.

A B C D E F G H I J K L M N O P Q R S T U V W X Y Z

Look at this example:

Example: If the code for **BAR** is **EDU**, what is the code for **NOW**? _____QRZ_____

13. If the code for **ALL** is **EPP**, what is the code for **MAP**? _____

14. If the code for **TENT** is **YJSY**, what is the code for **PART**? _____

15. If the code for **LEFT** is **NDHS**, what is **HNPS** the code for? _____

16. If the code for **PARK** is **NYPI**, what is the code for **WELL**? _____

17. If the code for **OBEY** is **NBFA**, what is **ZNOQB** the code for? _____

18. If the code for **PAINT** is **KZRMG**, what is the code for **TOUR**? _____

19. If the code for **GAPE** is **DXMB**, what is **EFKDB** the code for? _____

20. If the code for **CATCH** is **DCWGM**, what is the code for **PINK**? _____

21. If the code for **LUCKY** is **OFXPB**, what is **ORMVW** the code for? _____

22. If the code for **UNCLE** is **VPFPJ**, what is the code for **FUSSY**? _____

23. If the code for **MARCH** is **PWUYK**, what is **DIDOV** the code for? _____

24. If the code for **BOUND** is **AMRJY**, what is the code for **IDEAS**? _____

Practice Questions

Number-Word Codes

The number codes for three of these four words are listed in a random order. Work out the code to answer the questions.

OARS   ARMY   RAMS   ARMS

2145   1243   6125

25. Find the code for the word **ARMS**.   _____

26. Find the code for the word **ROAM**.   _____

27. Find the word that has the number code **5612**.   _____

HEAT   LATE   FEEL   FLEA

4612   3561   3665

28. Find the code for the word **FLEA**.   _____

29. Find the code for the word **HALL**.   _____

30. Find the word that has the number code **3126**.   _____

CORE   DOOR   ROAD   DEAR

2351   6324   1452

31. Find the code for the word **ROAD**.   _____

32. Find the code for the word **ORCA**.   _____

33. Find the word that has the number code **6314**.   _____

Practice Questions

SALT	SEAL	SELL	BALL
	3142	6144	3514

34. Find the code for the word **SALT**. _____

35. Find the code for the word **EAST**. _____

36. Find the word that has the number code **6532**. _____

GLAD	GAME	MALE	DEEM
	5324	5216	1236

37. Find the code for the word **DEEM**. _____

38. Find the code for the word **GALE**. _____

39. Find the word that has the number code **3624**. _____

LEAF	SEAT	FATE	EATS
	4256	1423	6425

40. Find the code for the word **LEAF**. _____

41. Find the code for the word **TALE**. _____

42. Find the word that has the number code **3265**. _____

PACE	NICE	CAPE	PINE
	2541	2631	4531

43. Find the code for the word **CAPE**. _____

44. Find the code for the word **PAIN**. _____

45. Find the word that has the number code **3641**. _____

Practice Questions

Read the information carefully, then use it to answer the question that follows. Underline the correct answer.

46. Sami, Jorge, Maya, Luke and Eve are choosing toppings for their burgers.

    Luke and Jorge have tomato on top of their burger. Maya is the only one who doesn't have onions. Everyone except Sami puts cheese on their burger. Only Maya and Jorge have bacon.

    Who has the **most** toppings on their burger? _____

47. Tori, Kim, Dennis, Ling and Uri are comparing all the places they have visited.

    Everyone has visited Manchester. Uri is the only one who hasn't been to Edinburgh. Dennis and Ling visited Cornwall together last year. Kim has also been to Cornwall, and she's the only person who has been to Bath. Tori and Kim have been to Kendal.

    Who has been to the **fewest** places? _____

48. Rashid, Charlie, Harry, Sona and Anita are discussing their hobbies.

    Only Charlie bakes. Everyone does swimming apart from Anita and Harry. Rashid, Charlie, Sona and Harry all play hockey. Anita goes to boxing classes with Sona. Only Anita plays the piano. Nobody except Sona does cycling.

    Who does the **most** hobbies? _____

49. Rob, Bianca, Violet, Chad and Georgia are discussing their favourite film genres.

    Rob and Bianca like comedy. Neither Georgia nor Chad like horror, but everyone else does. Everyone is a fan of romance films except for Rob. Georgia and Violet both like sci-fi. Bianca is the only one who enjoys action films.

    Who likes the **most** genres? _____

Practice Questions

50. Anwar, Monique, Wes, Hank and Shirley are all in a painting class together.

    Hank is the only person who is using purple paint. Monique, Wes and Anwar are all using black. Shirley is the only one who isn't using yellow paint. Everyone is using white in their paintings except for Anwar. Wes and Hank are not using any blue paint, but everyone else is.

    Who is using the **fewest** colours?   _____

51. James, William, Ella, Phoebe and Sasha are helping with jobs around the house.

    James and William both cleaned the bathroom. Ella tidied the kitchen and the lounge. Everyone cleaned the dining room except Sasha. Phoebe helped to tidy the lounge. Ella and James both cleaned the garage. Sasha was the only one who tidied the hall.

    Who helped out in the **most** rooms?   _____

52. Mhairi, Gwen, Anders, Emily and Shawn are bringing food to a birthday party.

    Mhairi and Gwen brought potato salad. Everyone except Gwen brought crisps and sandwiches. Anders brought sausage rolls, cookies and brownies. Emily supplied the birthday cake. Shawn brought brownies as well as pizza.

    Who brought the **most** food to the party?   _____

53. Philip, Victor, Theresa, Hector and Erin have gone to the market.

    Erin, Theresa and Hector bought oranges. Everyone bought apples and peaches except for Hector who only bought peaches. Philip bought bananas, grapes and pears. Hector also bought grapes and pears, as well as some strawberries.

    Who bought the **fewest** types of fruit?   _____

Practice Questions

Solve the Riddle

Read the information carefully, then use it to answer the question that follows. Underline the correct answer.

54. Luca, Helen, Tessa, Maren and Jasper are collecting shells on the beach. Luca collects the second highest number of shells. Helen collects fewer shells than Tessa. Jasper collects more shells than Luca.

Which one of the sentences below **must** be true?

A   Jasper collected the most shells.

B   Maren and Jasper collected the same number of shells.

C   Tessa didn't collect any shells.

D   Helen collected an odd number of shells.

E   Maren collected the fewest shells.

55. Naomi, Craig, Li, Petra and Maria are talking about their pets. Petra has twice as many pets as Li. Maria has one fewer pet than Petra. Li has two pets. Craig and Naomi both have the same number of pets as Maria.

Which one of the sentences below **cannot** be true?

A   Petra has four pets.

B   There are fifteen pets in total.

C   Maria has three dogs.

D   Craig and Naomi are siblings.

E   Naomi has fewer pets than Li.

56. Orla, John, Anza, Ellie and Imani are racing each other to the shops. Anza doesn't come fourth. Anza beats Orla. Ellie comes third. John reaches the shops before Anza.

Which one of the sentences below **cannot** be true?

A   John is the winner.

B   Orla beats Ellie.

C   John was one minute faster than Ellie.

D   Imani comes last.

E   Orla runs faster than Imani.

Practice Questions

57. Pascal, Jessie, Summer, Luke and Anthony are all on the same bus. Luke got on the bus at 5.45. Anthony got on the bus twenty minutes after Luke. Jessie got on ten minutes after Anthony. Pascal was the first one of them to get on the bus. Luke got on half an hour before Summer.

Which one of the sentences below **must** be true?

A   Pascal got on the bus ten minutes before Luke.

B   The bus was running late.

C   Anthony was the last person to get on the bus.

D   Pascal and Luke got on the bus together.

E   Summer and Jessie got on the bus at the same time.

58. Bella, Frankie, Ray, Denny and Gemma are sharing a plate of six apples and six pears. Bella ate an apple and a pear. Frankie ate two pears. Ray had one apple and two pears. Gemma ate three apples.

Which one of the sentences below **cannot** be true?

A   Gemma would have preferred a pear.

B   Denny ate two apples and a pear.

C   Frankie ate twice as many pears as Bella.

D   Denny had an apple.

E   All of the fruit was eaten.

59. Hazim, Rachel, Thandi, Ash and Kingsley are comparing their marks from their biology test. Thandi got the highest mark. Ash scored fifteen marks fewer than Thandi. Rachel scored 75, five marks more than Ash. Hazim came last with a score of 58.

Which one of the sentences below **must** be true?

A   Kingsley and Hazim came joint last.

B   Three of the children scored less than 70.

C   Ash got 80 marks.

D   Thandi scored 85 marks.

E   Kingsley failed the test.

Mixed Practice Tests

If you want to attempt each mixed practice test more than once, you will need to print **multiple-choice answer sheets** for these questions from our website — go to www.cgpbooks.co.uk/11plusanswersheets. If you'd prefer to answer them in standard write-in format, follow the instructions in the tests.

Give yourself **12 minutes** to complete this test. Write down your score in the box at the end.

Test 1

Underline two words, one from each set of brackets, that have the most opposite meaning. Look at this example:

Example: (confident <u>worried</u> annoyed) (assured <u>calm</u> elated)

1. (sudden relentless perpetual) (scarce momentary frequent)

2. (disobey intervene petition) (discharge comply ignore)

3. (timid thoughtful inquisitive) (uninterested secretive trusting)

4. (uninvolved passionate energetic) (critical apathetic reluctant)

Choose two words, one from each set of brackets, that complete the sentence in the most sensible way. Underline both words. Look at this example.

Example: Teacher is to (learn <u>school</u> books) as **nurse** is to (care medical <u>hospital</u>).

5. **Rugby** is to (pitch ball tackle) as **basketball** is to (net court round).

6. **Depart** is to (remain voyage fly) as **occupy** is to (live habitat vacate).

7. **Pea** is to (green pod vegetable) as **egg** is to (yolk shell hard).

8. **Abundance** is to (full plenty wealth) as **scarcity** is to (quantity shortage available).

Mixed Practice Tests

Find the missing number to complete each sum. Look at this example:

Example: 20 ÷ 4 = 2 + (?)

   A 1   **B** 2   **C** <u>3</u>   **D** 4   **E** 5

9. 30 + 12 = 49 – (?)

   A 3   **B** 5   **C** 6   **D** 7   **E** 11

10. 18 ÷ 2 = 3 + (?)

   A 4   **B** 6   **C** 8   **D** 10   **E** 13

11. 12 + 5 – 10 = 8 – (?)

   A 1   **B** 4   **C** 5   **D** 7   **E** 15

12. 8 × 4 + 14 = 51 – (?)

   A 3   **B** 5   **C** 7   **D** 17   **E** 23

The number codes for three of these four words are listed in a random order. Work out the code to answer the questions.

   MOAT   **HOME**   **MOTH**   **MEAT**

   2465   6531   6412

13. Find the code for the word **MOAT**.

   A 5413   **B** 6325   **C** 5341   **D** 6431   **E** 6412

14. Find the code for the word **TOME**.

   A 1462   **B** 3615   **C** 1465   **D** 2136   **E** 1356

15. Find the word that has the number code **1256**.

   A ATOM   **B** TEAM   **C** THAT   **D** HATE   **E** THEM

Mixed Practice Tests

In each sentence below, a four-letter word is hidden at the end of one word and the start of the next. Underline the part of the sentence that contains the hidden word. Look at the example below:

Example: Tia had more than enou<u>gh ear</u>rings.

　　　　A Tia had　**B** had more　**C** more than　**D** than enough　**E** <u>enough earrings</u>

(The hidden word is **hear**.)

16. The theatre exit was totally blocked.

　　A The theatre　　**B** theatre exit　　**C** exit was　　**D** was totally　　**E** totally blocked

17. We're glad you came after us.

　　A We're glad　　**B** glad you　　**C** you came　　**D** came after　　**E** after us

18. The grizzly bear chased the rabbit.

　　A The grizzly　　**B** grizzly bear　　**C** bear chased　　**D** chased the　　**E** the rabbit

19. The chef aired her apron outside.

　　A The chef　　**B** chef aired　　**C** aired her　　**D** her apron　　**E** apron outside

Read the information carefully, then use it to answer the question that follows. Underline the correct answer.

20. Tani, Frank, Earl, Ben and Amos all have posters on their bedroom wall.

Tani, Earl and Ben are the only ones who have a tiger poster. Everyone except Ben has a unicorn poster. Amos is the only one who has a car poster. Tani, Earl and Amos all have a dog poster. Frank is the only one who does not have a film poster.

Who has the **fewest** posters on their bedroom wall?

　　A　Tani　　　　**B**　Frank　　　**C**　Earl　　　　**D**　Ben　　　　**E**　Amos

Total (out of 20):

Mixed Practice Tests

Give yourself **12 minutes** to complete this test. Write down your score in the box at the end.

Test 2

Find the three-letter word that completes the word in capital letters, and so finishes the sentence in a sensible way. Look at this example:

Example: Marco **WED** a new bike for his birthday.

        A AND   **B** NET   **C** ANT   **D** END   **E** ERR

Answer: **ANT** (the complete word is **WANTED**)

---

1. Lottie **BDED** the plane and sat down in her seat.

    A AIM   **B** EAR   **C** ARE   **D** OIL   **E** OAR

2. We used lots of bubble wrap to protect the **FILE** contents of the box.

    A AGE   **B** RAN   **C** RAG   **D** APT   **E** ANY

3. We used a **SCIL** to draw lots of identical stars.

    A RAW   **B** TIN   **C** PET   **D** TEN   **E** PAN

4. Beata bought a bow and some arrows before she began **ARCY** lessons.

    A ARE   **B** HER   **C** TIN   **D** EAR   **E** TAN

Three of the words in each list are linked. Underline the two words that are not related to these three. Look at this example:

Example: lake   ocean   <u>shore</u>   stream   <u>bank</u>

---

5. habit   option   practice   routine   choice

6. textbook   fable   legend   fairytale   dictionary

7. luminous   searing   radiant   ignited   incandescent

8. nourished   satisfied   guzzled   devoured   gorged

Mixed Practice Tests

Find the number that completes the final set of numbers in the same way as the first two sets. Look at this example:

Example: 7 (11) 4   3 (15) 12   6 (?) 5

A 1   B 4   C <u>11</u>   D 19   E 30

9. 7 (12) 1   5 (8) 1   7 (?) 2

A 5   B 9   C 10   D 17   E 24

10. 12 (5) 3   8 (4) 4   3 (?) 6

A 2   B 3   C 6   D 15   E 17

11. 12 (1) 3   40 (2) 8   24 (?) 6

A 1   B 3   C 7   D 12   E 15

12. 8 (10) 6   6 (5) 5   5 (?) 4

A 2   B 4   C 5   D 7   E 13

Find the word that completes the third pair of words so that it follows the same pattern as the first two pairs. Look at this example:

Example: amiably may   brought rut   advised (?)

A aid   B <u>did</u>   C dad   D sea   E sad

13. hungry rung   courts tour   bridge (?)

A bred   B ride   C dire   D bide   E grid

14. stakes sets   ritual lair   leader (?)

A reel   B deal   C leer   D dear   E real

15. objects bets   impacts mats   repairs (?)

A rare   B spar   C ears   D errs   E pear

16. cleared deal   proudly your   seating (?)

A sage   B gate   C sing   D gain   E tags

Mixed Practice Tests

Find the pair of letters that continues each sequence in the best way.
Use the alphabet to help you.

A B C D E F G H I J K L M N O P Q R S T U V W X Y Z

Example: MZ   NY   OX   PW   (?)

       A OV   **B** RV   **C** QU   **D** <u>QV</u>   **E** RU

17. MM   OL   QJ   SG   UC   (?)

    A WZ   **B** WX   **C** XX   **D** VX   **E** WW

18. KI   LL   OJ   PM   SK   (?)

    A VN   **B** UM   **C** TN   **D** VM   **E** TO

19. TQ   WV   YA   ZF   ZK   (?)

    A YO   **B** AP   **C** ZO   **D** ZP   **E** YP

20. LG   NE   RD   TB   XA   (?)

    A ZY   **B** ZZ   **C** BZ   **D** BY   **E** ZA

Total (out of 20): ☐

Mixed Practice Tests

Mixed Practice Tests

Give yourself **12 minutes** to complete this test. Write down your score in the box at the end.

Test 3

> Underline two words, one from each set of brackets, that have the most similar meaning. Look at this example:
>
> **Example:** (isolated <u>rural</u> green)   (wild quiet <u>rustic</u>)

1. (abnormal grotesque intriguing)   (abrupt outlandish improbable)

2. (attack confiscate seize)   (commandeer ransack control)

3. (captivating unfamiliar bewildering)   (odd distressing mystifying)

4. (unnerve distract incite)   (confound surprise perturb)

> Find the letter that will finish the first word and start the second word of each pair. The same letter must be used for both pairs. Look at this example:
>
> **Example:** bon (?) one   her (?) ear
>
>   **A** l   **B** n   **C** <u>d</u>   **D** o   **E** p

5. los (?) ip   sea (?) ask

   A e   **B** p   **C** t   **D** l   **E** h

6. cur (?) ore   stu (?) an

   A m   **B** t   **C** n   **D** b   **E** c

7. sol (?) we   temp (?) ath

   A e   **B** o   **C** d   **D** p   **E** b

8. drie (?) eal   bia (?) igh

   A h   **B** l   **C** m   **D** d   **E** s

Mixed Practice Tests

Each letter stands for a number. Work out the answer to each sum as a letter.

Example: A = 1, B = 4, C = 7, D = 8, E = 11
        C + B = (?)

A A   **B** B   **C** C   **D** D   **E** E̲

9. A = 1, B = 2, C = 4, D = 7, E = 8
        B × C ÷ E = (?)

   A A   **B** B   **C** C   **D** D   **E** E

10. A = 1, B = 5, C = 10, D = 14, E = 20
        E ÷ B + C = (?)

   A A   **B** B   **C** C   **D** D   **E** E

11. A = 2, B = 3, C = 8, D = 13, E = 15
        A × B + E − D = (?)

   A A   **B** B   **C** C   **D** D   **E** E

12. A = 6, B = 8, C = 9, D = 18, E = 35
        D ÷ A × C + B = (?)

   A A   **B** B   **C** C   **D** D   **E** E

Mark a word from the first set, followed by a word from the second set,
that go together to form a new word. Look at this example:

Example: (bee miss o̲v̲e̲r̲) (herd c̲o̲m̲e̲ leave)   (the new word is 'overcome')

13. (all past for)   (most mat time)

14. (are how set)   (self side led)

15. (for seem tire)   (less dome most)

16. (wave ice paw)   (late sing red)

Mixed Practice Tests

Each question uses a different code.
Use the alphabet to help you work out the answer to each question.

A B C D E F G H I J K L M N O P Q R S T U V W X Y Z

Example: If the code for **BIKE** is **ELNH**, what is **EDVLQ** the code for?

    A BOOST   **B** BACON   **C** BRAIN   **D** <u>BASIN</u>   **E** BATON

17. If the code for **ZEST** is **DZWO**, what is the code for **JAZZ**?

    A NFDV   **B** NVDU   **C** FOVE   **D** OEDV   **E** FWVV

18. If the code for **DINT** is **WRMG**, what is the code for **INNER**?

    A RMLXI   **B** QMMVI   **C** RMMVI   **D** QWWDS   **E** RLLWJ

19. If the code for **MIMIC** is **NILGZ**, what is **QIDBB** the code for?

    A PIANO   **B** NIECE   **C** PIERS   **D** PIECE   **E** NIGHT

Read the information carefully, then use it to answer the question that follows. Underline the correct answer.

20. Ana, Teddy, Max, Nina and Darcy are comparing how many siblings they have.
    Ana has twice as many siblings as Teddy. Darcy has one more sibling than Teddy.
    Teddy has one brother and one sister. Max has more siblings than Darcy.

    Which one of the sentences below **must** be true?

    A   Ana has two brothers and two sisters.

    B   Max has at least four siblings.

    C   Nina is an only child.

    D   Teddy has the most siblings.

    E   Darcy has three brothers.

Total (out of 20):

Mixed Practice Tests

Give yourself **12 minutes** to complete this test. Write down your score in the box at the end.

Choose the word that has a similar meaning to the words in both sets of brackets.
Underline your answer. Look at this example:

Example: (wrap package) (fill load)   envelop carton <u>pack</u> crate store

1. (corrupt unethical) (putrid decaying)   fetid wily fraudulent crooked rotten

2. (squash squeeze)   (throng crowd)   crush mob group hoard push

3. (sincere heartfelt)   (profound weighty)   difficult heavy truthful serious potent

4. (cure treatment)   (solve right)   medicine remedy salve correct result

Remove one letter from the first word and add it to the second word to make two new
words. Do not change the order of the other letters. Underline the letter that moves.

Example: short   our

A s   **B** <u>h</u>   **C** o   **D** r   **E** t

(The new words are **sort** and **hour**.)

5. defer   law
    A d   **B** e   **C** f   **D** e   **E** r

6. rally   eve
    A r   **B** a   **C** l   **D** l   **E** y

7. fused   boy
    A f   **B** u   **C** s   **D** e   **E** d

8. chart   sip
    A c   **B** h   **C** a   **D** r   **E** t

Mixed Practice Tests

Find the number that continues each sequence in the best way. Look at this example:

Example: 3, 6, 9, 12, (?)

      A 14   **B** <u>15</u>   **C** 17   **D** 19   **E** 21

9. 61, 63, 67, 73, 81, (?)

    A 83   **B** 87   **C** 91   **D** 97   **E** 93

10. 19, 23, 13, 33, 7, 43, (?)

    A 1   **B** 3   **C** 13   **D** 26   **E** 53

11. 30, 32, 33, 33, 32, (?)

    A 28   **B** 30   **C** 32   **D** 33   **E** 35

12. 1, 28, 2, 24, 4, 20, (?)

    A 6   **B** 8   **C** 12   **D** 16   **E** 18

The words in the second set follow the same pattern as the words in the first set. Underline the missing word to complete the second set. Look at the example below.

Example: pour (rot) tone   curt (?) rasp

      A sat   **B** pat   **C** rut   **D** <u>tar</u>   **E** car

13. base (same) sums   crib (_____) deal

    A idea   **B** dear   **C** lace   **D** drab   **E** bale

14. eager (mare) games   agape (_____) evade

    A aged   **B** gave   **C** deep   **D** aped   **E** gape

15. lair (rail) brim   dame (_____) epic

    A pied   **B** deem   **C** pace   **D** dice   **E** paid

16. boss (rose) rice   upon (_____) shut

    A posh   **B** shop   **C** spot   **D** push   **E** stop

Mixed Practice Tests

Find the pair of letters that completes each sentence in the most sensible way. Use the alphabet to help you.

A B C D E F G H I J K L M N O P Q R S T U V W X Y Z

Example: **FH** is to **HJ** as **PR** is to (?)

      A RP   **B** NL   **C** <u>RT</u>   **D** RS   **E** NP

17. **OH** is to **JI** as **PI** is to (?)

    A HI   **B** KH   **C** KJ   **D** JG   **E** KI

18. **NA** is to **MZ** as **KJ** is to (?)

    A QO   **B** NR   **C** QQ   **D** PQ   **E** PR

19. **XG** is to **YD** as **FR** is to (?)

    A GQ   **B** GP   **C** GO   **D** GL   **E** JL

20. **HQ** is to **SJ** as **SV** is to (?)

    A HE   **B** FE   **C** GE   **D** FC   **E** HF

Total (out of 20):

CGP

There are **multiple-choice answer sheets** for these questions on our website —
go to www.cgpbooks.co.uk/11plusanswersheets. If you want to attempt each paper
more than once, you will need to print a separate answer sheet for each attempt.

11+ Verbal Reasoning
For Ages 10-11
Practice Paper 1
For GL Assessment

Read the following:

Do not start the test until you are told to do so.

1. This is a multiple-choice test.

2. There are 80 questions and you will have 50 minutes to do the test.

3. You should mark your answer to each question in pencil on the answer sheet
   you've printed from www.cgpbooks.co.uk/11plusanswersheets.

4. You should only mark one answer for each question, unless the question instruction says
   otherwise. To mark your answer, draw a straight line through the rectangle next to the option
   you have chosen. If you make a mistake, rub it out and mark your new answer clearly.

5. Make sure you keep your place on the answer sheet and mark your
   answer in the box that has the same number as the question.

6. Do as many questions as you can. If you get stuck on a question, choose the answer
   that you think is most likely to be correct, then move on to the next question.

7. You should do any rough working on a separate piece of paper.

Work carefully, but go as quickly as you can.

Find the three-letter word that completes the word in capital letters, and so finishes the sentence in a sensible way.

Example   It took Gemma five **HS** to run a marathon.

     A APE   **B** EAR   **C** OUR   **D** ONE   **E** AND

Answer   **OUR** (the complete word is **HOURS**)

1 After years apart, Allie was **REUED** with her best friend.

     A SUM   **B** NET   **C** ONE   **D** VOW   **E** NIT

2 My grandma was **AGT** at how messy my room was.

     A ASK   **B** HAS   **C** SAD   **D** APE   **E** ROW

3 Din usually **REPS** quickly to the letters from his pen pal.

     A SIT   **B** LAY   **C** SON   **D** LIE   **E** TRY

4 The doctor gave an **ANTIE** to the patient who had been poisoned.

     A AID   **B** RAN   **C** DOT   **D** HEM   **E** ATE

5 My dog **LHES** going to the vet — he whines all the way there.

     A EAR   **B** RUE   **C** AIR   **D** OAT   **E** OFT

- -

Three of the words in each list are linked. Find the two words that are **not** related to these three and mark them **both** on the answer sheet.

Example   **A** friend   **B** help   **C** assist   **D** playmate   **E** aid

Answer   **friend** and **playmate**

6 **A** crops   **B** wheat   **C** oats   **D** shears   **E** barley

7 **A** feathers   **B** cotton   **C** scales   **D** fabric   **E** fur

8 **A** tend   **B** harvest   **C** gather   **D** nurture   **E** reap

9 **A** truck   **B** trailer   **C** cart   **D** car   **E** van

10 **A** ridge   **B** dent   **C** hollow   **D** cavity   **E** hill

Turn over to the next page

11 **A** appalled **B** baffled **C** horrified **D** bewildered **E** dismayed

12 **A** praise **B** compliment **C** commend **D** please **E** accept

---

Find the pair of letters that completes each sentence in the most sensible way.
Use the alphabet to help you.

ABCDEFGHIJKLMNOPQRSTUVWXYZ

Example   BD is to DF as FI is to (?)

   A HK   **B** HJ   **C** GK   **D** FE   **E** HL

Answer   HK

13 TV is to WU as SJ is to (?)
   A VF   **B** UG   **C** VI   **D** UI   **E** VJ

14 JM is to QN as LR is to (?)
   A JI   **B** OL   **C** HI   **D** OI   **E** OJ

15 GU is to EZ as MT is to (?)
   A KY   **B** LX   **C** LY   **D** LA   **E** OY

16 NK is to OE as OR is to (?)
   A MN   **B** PL   **C** RJ   **D** NL   **E** PK

17 IT is to RG as GQ is to (?)
   A TH   **B** TJ   **C** SH   **D** SJ   **E** TL

Find the number that continues each sequence in the best way.

Example   2, 6, 10, 14, (?)

   A 14   **B** 16   **C** 18   **D** 20   **E** 24

Answer   18

18 4, 5, 9, 14, 23, (?)
   A 24   **B** 32   **C** 35   **D** 37   **E** 40

19   45, 44, 41, 36, 29, (?)

     A 16   **B** 18   **C** 19   **D** 20   **E** 22

20   2, 5, 4, 11, 8, 17, (?)

     A 14   **B** 16   **C** 20   **D** 23   **E** 28

21   9, 16, 17, 15, 25, 14, (?)

     A 13   **B** 16   **C** 26   **D** 31   **E** 33

22   53, 52, 52, 53, 55, (?)

     A 53   **B** 55   **C** 58   **D** 60   **E** 62

23   64, 45, 16, 46, 4, 47, (?)

     A 1   **B** 2   **C** 8   **D** 32   **E** 48

Find the word that completes the third pair of words so that it follows the same pattern as the first two pairs.

Example   (dear ear)   (twin win)   (rate [?])

         A rat   **B** eat   **C** tar   **D** ate   **E** tea

Answer   ate

24   (engine inn)   (caused sea)   (reward [?])

     A awe   **B** red   **C** are   **D** wed   **E** war

25   (sure rue)   (camp map)   (past [?])

     A sap   **B** tap   **C** apt   **D** sat   **E** pat

26   (fellows slow)   (legends send)   (hearing [?])

     A near   **B** gain   **C** grin   **D** rein   **E** gear

27   (antenna tan)   (imagery aim)   (intends [?])

     A tin   **B** ten   **C** din   **D** sit   **E** sin

28   (rounded rude)   (chopped cope)   (broader [?])

     A bode   **B** robe   **C** drab   **D** bred   **E** boar

Turn over to the next page

Find **two** words, one from each set of brackets, that go together to form a new word.
Mark **both** words on the answer sheet.

Example   (else fire tram)   (sit wear work)

         A else   **X** sit

         B fire   **Y** wear

         C tram   **Z** work

Answer   **fire** and **work** (the new word is **firework**)

29 (art prod in)   (take fact cure)

    A art   **X** take

    B prod   **Y** fact

    C in   **Z** cure

30 (under con off)   (soul tone ten)

    A under   **X** soul

    B con   **Y** tone

    C off   **Z** ten

31 (bag news pass)   (by ward age)

    A bag   **X** by

    B news   **Y** ward

    C pass   **Z** age

32 (real ask plea)   (less sing ice)

    A real   **X** less

    B ask   **Y** sing

    C plea   **Z** ice

33 (bear back he)   (lash ring down)

    A bear   **X** lash

    B back   **Y** ring

    C he   **Z** down

Find **two** words, one from each set of brackets, that have the most **opposite** meaning. Mark **both** words on the answer sheet.

Example   (angry nervous irritating)   (relaxed tired satisfied)

        A angry   **X** relaxed

        B nervous   **Y** tired

        C irritating   **Z** satisfied

Answer   **nervous** and **relaxed**

34 (invert justify concede)   (deny avert recede)

        A invert   **X** deny

        B justify   **Y** avert

        C concede   **Z** recede

35 (liberate transfer confine)   (ransom prevent detain)

        A liberate   **X** ransom

        B transfer   **Y** prevent

        C confine   **Z** detain

36 (agile active adamant)   (reluctant stagnant faltering)

        A agile   **X** reluctant

        B active   **Y** stagnant

        C adamant   **Z** faltering

37 (certainty sense insensitivity)   (tact tolerance wisdom)

        A certainty   **X** tact

        B sense   **Y** tolerance

        C insensitivity   **Z** wisdom

38 (dissuade provoke undermine)   (appease attract apologise)

        A dissuade   **X** appease

        B provoke   **Y** attract

        C undermine   **Z** apologise

Turn over to the next page

Each question uses a different code.
Use the alphabet to help you work out the answer to each question.

A B C D E F G H I J K L M N O P Q R S T U V W X Y Z

Example   If the code for **FISH** is **JMWL**, what is **TPERX** the code for?

A PRUNE   **B** PLANE   **C** HOMES   **D** PLANT   **E** HIDES

Answer   **PLANT**

39   If the code for **ABLE** is **FGQJ**, what is **QNSP** the code for?
A LINE   **B** VICE   **C** LIFE   **D** LINK   **E** VOLE

40   If the code for **SPIN** is **POFM**, what is the code for **NAME**?
A QBPF   **B** KZJD   **C** QZPD   **D** KBJD   **E** KYJF

41   If the code for **TIME** is **GRNV**, what is the code for **RELIC**?
A IVMTP   **B** IRMYS   **C** IVORX   **D** EZMRX   **E** IVPSX

42   If the code for **TINT** is **PMJX**, what is **WPHSS** the code for?
A ALLOW   **B** CANES   **C** ALLOY   **D** DELAY   **E** YACHT

43   If the code for **GLARE** is **HNDVJ**, what is the code for **LIES**?
A KLHW   **B** MHFW   **C** MKHX   **D** KMHW   **E** MKHW

44   If the code for **TALES** is **GZOVH**, what is **HLMT** the code for?
A TONG   **B** SUNG   **C** SAME   **D** SONG   **E** SOUP

45   If the code for **EVENT** is **EUCKP**, what is the code for **TENOR**?
A TDPRV   **B** SGQQW   **C** TDLLN   **D** SCKLM   **E** TDLKM

- -

Read the information carefully, then use it to answer the question that follows.

46   Steven, Astrid, Lia, Jimmy and Hamid are buying snacks at a supermarket.
Astrid and Hamid each buy crackers. Steven and Lia are the only two who buy grapes.
Everyone apart from Astrid buys a chocolate bar. Nobody except Jimmy buys berries.
Lia, Steven and Hamid all buy carrot sticks.

Who buys the **fewest** snacks?

A Steven   **B** Astrid   **C** Lia   **D** Jimmy   **E** Hamid

47 Emma, Ren, Lehana, Marvin and Annie went snorkelling.
Only Lehana came across a jellyfish.
Everyone apart from Ren and Lehana saw a starfish.
All of the children except for Marvin saw a clownfish.
The two children who saw a stingray were Emma and Ren.
Marvin was the only one who saw a sea turtle.

Who saw the **most** sea creatures?

A Emma   **B** Ren   **C** Lehana   **D** Marvin   **E** Annie

---

Find the pair of letters that continues each sequence in the best way.
Use the alphabet to help you.

A B C D E F G H I J K L M N O P Q R S T U V W X Y Z

Example   HN   HO   IP   IQ   (?)

A JQ   **B** JS   **C** HM   **D** IN   **E** JR

Answer   **JR**

48 ET   CR   DU   BS   CV   (?)
A AT   **B** ET   **C** AV   **D** AX   **E** YT

49 GI   FH   DJ   CI   AK   (?)
A YJ   **B** ZL   **C** YI   **D** ZJ   **E** YM

50 ES   FW   GZ   HB   IC   (?)
A JD   **B** KC   **C** JB   **D** IC   **E** JC

51 OM   RP   WR   ZS   ES   (?)
A HT   **B** HR   **C** JS   **D** JR   **E** HS

52 IW   JU   JQ   IO   GK   (?)
A MI   **B** DI   **C** EI   **D** CD   **E** ID

Turn over to the next page

The number codes for three of these four words are listed in a random order.
Work out the code to answer the questions.

GEAR   FAIR   RAGE   RARE

6325   4135   5341

53 Find the code for the word **RARE**.

   A 5254   **B** 2624   **C** 5351   **D** 6364   **E** 4561

54 Find the code for the word **REEF**.

   A 4336   **B** 5116   **C** 5224   **D** 6221   **E** 5114

55 Find the word that has the number code **6251**.

   A FEAR   **B** RIFE   **C** FAIR   **D** FIRE   **E** REAR

The number codes for three of these four words are listed in a random order.
Work out the code to answer the questions.

LANE   TEEN   TONE   NOTE

4362   1542   6342

56 Find the code for the word **LANE**.

   A 6543   **B** 1542   **C** 1436   **D** 3251   **E** 1462

57 Find the code for the word **NEAT**.

   A 4263   **B** 4516   **C** 6345   **D** 4256   **E** 3615

58 Find the word that has the number code **1254**.

   A NEAT   **B** LATE   **C** LEAN   **D** TEAL   **E** TOLL

Remove one letter from the first word and add it to the second word to make two new words.
Do not change the order of the other letters. Mark the letter that moves on the answer sheet.

Example   alone   net

            A a   **B** l   **C** o   **D** n   **E** e

Answer   a (the new words are **lone** and **neat**)

59 event   new

   A e   **B** v   **C** e   **D** n   **E** t

60 where ace
    A w   **B** h   **C** e   **D** r   **E** e

61 plead sun
    A p   **B** l   **C** e   **D** a   **E** d

62 gable red
    A g   **B** a   **C** b   **D** l   **E** e

63 range tow
    A r   **B** a   **C** n   **D** g   **E** e

Each letter stands for a number. Work out the answer to each sum as a letter.

Example   A = 3, B = 4, C = 7, D = 10, E = 11
        B + A = (?)

        A A   **B** B   **C** C   **D** D   **E** E

Answer   **C**

64 A = 3, B = 9, C = 13, D = 14, E = 38
    A × B − C = (?)

    A A   **B** B   **C** C   **D** D   **E** E

65 A = 1, B = 2, C = 4, D = 8, E = 16
    B × E ÷ C = (?)

    A A   **B** B   **C** C   **D** D   **E** E

66 A = 4, B = 5, C = 9, D = 10, E = 16
    E ÷ A + D − C = (?)

    A A   **B** B   **C** C   **D** D   **E** E

67 A = 3, B = 4, C = 8, D = 11, E = 15
    C + B ÷ A + D = (?)

    A A   **B** B   **C** C   **D** D   **E** E

68 A = 2, B = 4, C = 10, D = 20, E = 30
    C × A + D ÷ B = (?)

    A A   **B** B   **C** C   **D** D   **E** E

Turn over to the next page

Find the number that completes the final set of numbers in the same way as the first two sets.

Example   2 (6) 3   4 (28) 7   2 (?) 9

           A 1   **B** 4   **C** 9   **D** 18   **E** 35

Answer   **18**

69 8 (20) 7   6 (12) 1   5 (?) 3
       A 2   **B** 4   **C** 8   **D** 13   **E** 14

70 35 (2) 7   36 (6) 4   8 (?) 2
       A 1   **B** 2   **C** 4   **D** 6   **E** 8

71 4 (12) 9   3 (7) 7   3 (?) 5
       A 2   **B** 5   **C** 6   **D** 9   **E** 15

72 7 (3) 6   7 (4) 5   9 (?) 4
       A 2   **B** 3   **C** 5   **D** 6   **E** 7

73 28 (1) 4   24 (2) 3   18 (?) 2
       A 1   **B** 3   **C** 6   **D** 9   **E** 16

Find the letter that will finish the first word and start the second word of each pair.
The same letter must be used for both pairs.

Example   dar (?) ap   edi (?) alk

           A e   **B** l   **C** m   **D** t   **E** w

Answer   **t**

74 stin (?) ick   tre (?) eep
       A t   **B** e   **C** s   **D** k   **E** p

75 use (?) ail   clea (?) ust
       A d   **B** n   **C** r   **D** s   **E** t

76 date (?) ue   ree (?) aze
       A s   **B** d   **C** r   **D** h   **E** m

77 swa (?) ear   shin (?) ank

   A b   **B** p   **C** n   **D** r   **E** y

78 loa (?) in   gol (?) ee

   A d   **B** g   **C** p   **D** f   **E** l

Read the information carefully, then use it to answer the question that follows.

79 Harvey, Angus, Polly, Taylor and Olga all took part in a football tournament.
The team with the most points came first. Polly's team got more points than Taylor's team.
Harvey's team came third. Olga's team finished with more points than Polly's team.
Taylor's team didn't come last.

If these statements are true, only one of the sentences below **must** be true. Which one?

   A Angus's team scored more points than Taylor's team.

   B Polly's team didn't come second.

   C Harvey's team scored twenty goals.

   D Olga's team scored more points than Taylor's team.

   E Angus's team came fourth.

80 Meena, Lucy, Albert, Harper and Camila all went to see a play. The play started at 7pm.
Albert arrived at the theatre thirty minutes after Camila. Lucy got there right after Albert.
Harper was fourth to arrive. Meena arrived 15 minutes before the start.
Camila arrived 45 minutes before Meena.

If these statements are true, only one of the sentences below **must** be true. Which one?

   A Harper arrived five minutes before Meena.

   B Meena had an aisle seat.

   C Albert was the third person to arrive.

   D Camila arrived at 6.30pm.

   E Lucy arrived after Camila.

End of test

There are **multiple-choice answer sheets** for these questions on our website —
go to www.cgpbooks.co.uk/11plusanswersheets. If you want to attempt each paper
more than once, you will need to print a separate answer sheet for each attempt.

11+ Verbal Reasoning
For Ages 10-11
Practice Paper 2

For GL Assessment

Read the following:

Do not start the test until you are told to do so.

1. This is a multiple-choice test.

2. There are 80 questions and you will have 50 minutes to do the test.

3. You should mark your answer to each question in pencil on the answer sheet
    you've printed from www.cgpbooks.co.uk/11plusanswersheets.

4. You should only mark one answer for each question, unless the question instruction says
    otherwise. To mark your answer, draw a straight line through the rectangle next to the option
    you have chosen. If you make a mistake, rub it out and mark your new answer clearly.

5. Make sure you keep your place on the answer sheet and mark your
    answer in the box that has the same number as the question.

6. Do as many questions as you can. If you get stuck on a question, choose the answer
    that you think is most likely to be correct, then move on to the next question.

7. You should do any rough working on a separate piece of paper.

Work carefully, but go as quickly as you can.

Find the pair of letters that continues each sequence in the best way.
Use the alphabet to help you.

A B C D E F G H I J K L M N O P Q R S T U V W X Y Z

Example   HN   HO   IP   IQ   (?)

   A JQ   **B** JS   **C** HM   **D** IN   **E** JR

Answer   **JR**

1   EM   HN   JO   KP   KQ   (?)
   A LQ   **B** IR   **C** JR   **D** JP   **E** LR

2   YO   AM   CL   EL   GM   (?)
   A IO   **B** JP   **C** EO   **D** IP   **E** IQ

3   UD   RB   PZ   OX   OV   (?)
   A PW   **B** OX   **C** NV   **D** PT   **E** NT

4   TF   QA   PW   MT   LR   (?)
   A KR   **B** IP   **C** IQ   **D** JQ   **E** JR

5   IX   EY   BA   ZD   YH   (?)
   A XN   **B** YM   **C** YN   **D** ZI   **E** XM

- -

The words in the second set follow the same pattern as the words in the first set.
Find the missing word to complete the second set.

Example   film (fit) tag   rugs (?) net

   A get   **B** set   **C** run   **D** sun   **E** gut

Answer   **run**

6   bake (beak) mire   sunk (?) boat
   A soak   **B** task   **C** stub   **D** stun   **E** tuna

7   prim (mope) poem   ache (?) helm
   A heel   **B** each   **C** meal   **D** heal   **E** male

8   begin (dine) imbed   heart (?) actor
   A rate   **B** tear   **C** race   **D** rote   **E** tact

Turn over to the next page

9 crazy (maze) teams   aisle (?) beats

    A tile   **B** ease   **C** teal   **D** eats   **E** tale

10 boar (crab) race   does (?) plus

    A soup   **B** sole   **C** used   **D** uses   **E** soul

---

Find **two** words, one from each set of brackets, that have the most **opposite** meaning. Mark **both** words on the answer sheet.

Example (angry nervous irritating) (relaxed tired satisfied)

    A angry   **X** relaxed

    B nervous   **Y** tired

    C irritating   **Z** satisfied

Answer   **nervous** and **relaxed**

11 (amplify improve bolster) (negate degenerate fall)

    A amplify   **X** negate

    B improve   **Y** degenerate

    C bolster   **Z** fall

12 (noticeable faded dappled) (imperceptible distant suggestible)

    A noticeable   **X** imperceptible

    B faded   **Y** distant

    C dappled   **Z** suggestible

13 (ruined destructive cruel) (cautious agreeable beneficial)

    A ruined   **X** cautious

    B destructive   **Y** agreeable

    C cruel   **Z** beneficial

14 (impairment failing ignorance) (educating understanding maturity)

    A impairment   **X** educating

    B failing   **Y** understanding

    C ignorance   **Z** maturity

15 (accuracy honesty correction) (duplicity inability fault)

    A accuracy   **X** duplicity

    B honesty   **Y** inability

    C correction   **Z** fault

In each sentence below a four-letter word is hidden at the end of one word and the start of the next. Mark the part of the sentence that contains the hidden word on the answer sheet.

Example   Some alligators like eating fresh fruit.

A Some alligators   **B** alligators like   **C** like eating   **D** eating fresh   **E** fresh fruit

Answer   **Some alligators** (the hidden word is **meal**)

16 Rory's new kitten doesn't like strangers.

A Rory's new   **B** new kitten   **C** kitten doesn't   **D** doesn't like   **E** like strangers

17 The smell was coming from over here.

A The smell   **B** smell was   **C** was coming   **D** from over   **E** over here

18 I had to undo several tricky knots.

A I had   **B** to undo   **C** undo several   **D** several tricky   **E** tricky knots

19 A note arrived for Nina today.

A A note   **B** note arrived   **C** arrived for   **D** for Nina   **E** Nina today

20 Ron plays the violin every afternoon.

A Ron plays   **B** plays the   **C** the violin   **D** violin every   **E** every afternoon

21 Leo changed the channel several times.

A Leo changed   **B** changed the   **C** the channel   **D** channel several **E** several times

---

Remove one letter from the first word and add it to the second word to make two new words. Do not change the order of the other letters. Mark the letter that moves on the answer sheet.

Example   alone   net

A a   **B** l   **C** o   **D** n   **E** e

Answer   **a** (the new words are **lone** and **neat**)

22 bread   eat

A b   **B** r   **C** e   **D** a   **E** d

23 solve   doe

A s   **B** o   **C** l   **D** v   **E** e

24 rapid   our

A r   **B** a   **C** p   **D** i   **E** d

Turn over to the next page

25 brake   tip

    A b   **B** r   **C** a   **D** k   **E** e

26 gripe   rag

    A g   **B** r   **C** i   **D** p   **E** e

Find **two** words, one from each set of brackets, that go together to form a new word.
Mark **both** words on the answer sheet.

Example   (else fire tram)   (sit wear work)

               A else   **X** sit

               B fire   **Y** wear

               C tram   **Z** work

Answer   **fire** and **work** (the new word is **firework**)

27   (stag access habit)   (age able act)

     A stag   **X** age

     B access   **Y** able

     C habit   **Z** act

28   (cape per tree)   (sent son able)

     A cape   **X** sent

     B per   **Y** son

     C tree   **Z** able

29   (treat part bet)   (meant near ray)

     A treat   **X** meant

     B part   **Y** near

     C bet   **Z** ray

30   (plain start miss)   (led nest form)

     A plain   **X** led

     B start   **Y** nest

     C miss   **Z** form

31   (isle imp enter)   (lie act and)

     A isle   **X** lie

     B imp   **Y** act

     C enter   **Z** and

Find the number that continues each sequence in the best way.

Example   2, 6, 10, 14, (?)

           A 14   **B** 16   **C** 18   **D** 20   **E** 24

Answer   **18**

32 26, 31, 38, 47, 58, (?)
    A 63   **B** 65   **C** 69   **D** 71   **E** 73

33 55, 80, 47, 20, 39, 5, (?)
    A 4   **B** 21   **C** 31   **D** 34   **E** 35

34 49, 4, 54, 12, 59, 36, (?)
    A 39   **B** 41   **C** 48   **D** 61   **E** 64

35 9, 14, 18, 21, 23, (?)
    A 24   **B** 25   **C** 26   **D** 27   **E** 28

36 40, 27, 36, 9, 32, 3, (?)
    A 1   **B** 18   **C** 28   **D** 29   **E** 35

37 4, 4, 6, 16, 8, 64, (?)
    A 8   **B** 10   **C** 12   **D** 20   **E** 32

Find the word that completes the third pair of words so that it follows the same pattern as the first two pairs.

Example   (dear ear)   (twin win)   (rate [?])

           A rat   **B** eat   **C** tar   **D** ate   **E** tea

Answer   **ate**

38 (jointly lint)   (eclipse slip)   (reached [?])
    A ache   **B** heed   **C** dear   **D** head   **E** each

39 (sending dens)   (further turf)   (routine [?])
    A rote   **B** tone   **C** tour   **D** tune   **E** rune

Turn over to the next page

136

40 (terrain rein)   (balance lace)   (belongs [?])

A song   B legs   C snob   D logs   E lose

41 (throat oath)   (stream east)   (angles [?])

A seal   B lean   C lane   D lags   E sang

42 (derived veer)   (brother hero)   (partner [?])

A near   B trap   C rant   D part   E nape

- -

Each letter stands for a number. Work out the answer to each sum as a letter.

Example   A = 3, B = 4, C = 7, D = 10, E = 11
$$B + A = (?)$$

A A   **B** B   **C** C   **D** D   **E** E

Answer   C

43   A = 4, B = 5, C = 7, D = 25, E = 27
$$B \times A + C = (?)$$

A A   **B** B   **C** C   **D** D   **E** E

44   A = 1, B = 3, C = 5, D = 7, E = 16
$$C + E \div B = (?)$$

A A   **B** B   **C** C   **D** D   **E** E

45   A = 2, B = 3, C = 5, D = 10, E = 40
$$E \div D + B - A = (?)$$

A A   **B** B   **C** C   **D** D   **E** E

46   A = 2, B = 5, C = 10, D = 12, E = 20
$$E \div B + C - D = (?)$$

A A   **B** B   **C** C   **D** D   **E** E

47   A = 1, B = 2, C = 3, D = 5, E = 8
$$D \times C + A \div B = (?)$$

A A   **B** B   **C** C   **D** D   **E** E

Read the information carefully, then use it to answer the question that follows.

48 Kiara, Alice, Vera, Bella and Irem are putting toppings on their pancakes.
Irem and Vera both sprinkle sugar on their pancakes. Bella and Alice cover their pancakes in jam. Kiara is the only one to add whipped cream. Only Bella doesn't add chocolate chips. Irem and Kiara both add a squirt of lemon juice.

Which child puts the **fewest** toppings on their pancake?

A Kiara   B Alice   C Vera   D Bella   E Irem

49 Danny, Mila, Lexi, Jake and Sienna all took part in their school's sports day.
Lexi, Mila and Sienna all did the egg and spoon race.
Jake was the only one to compete in the long jump.
Everybody apart from Danny took part in the relay race.
Danny, Jake and Mila competed in the 100m sprint.
Jake and Lexi were the only two who did the three-legged race.

Who competed in the **most** events?

A Danny   B Mila   C Lexi   D Jake   E Sienna

- -

Choose **two** words, one from each set of brackets, that complete the sentence in the most sensible way. Mark **both** words on the answer sheet.

Example   **Fire** is to (burn   crackle   flame) as **phone** is to (talk   answer   ring).

         A burn   X talk

         B crackle   Y answer

         C flame   Z ring

Answer   **crackle** and **ring**

50 **Lead** is to (pencil   follow   metal) as **ink** is to (pen   chalk   draw).

         A pencil   X pen

         B follow   Y chalk

         C metal   Z draw

51 **Rocket** is to (fire   space   travel) as **submarine** is to (deep   propeller   ocean).

         A fire   X deep

         B space   Y propeller

         C travel   Z ocean

52 **Dismantle** is to (remove   build   part) as **create** is to (destroy   art   originate).

         A remove   X destroy

         B build   Y art

         C part   Z originate

Turn over to the next page

53 **Freeze** is to (frost   crystal   solidify) as **thaw** is to (melt   heat   boil).

A frost   X melt

B crystal   Y heat

C solidify   Z boil

54 **Order** is to (obedience   demand   rules) as **disorder** is to (rebellion   lax   random).

A obedience   X rebellion

B demand   Y lax

C rules   Z random

The number codes for three of these four words are listed in a random order.
Work out the code to answer the questions.

FUEL   FOUR   RULE   FREE

1356   4365   1234

55 Find the code for the word **RULE**.

A 4351   B 4365   C 2314   D 4536   E 1254

56 Find the code for the word **ROOF**.

A 2335   B 4221   C 5332   D 4551   E 4662

57 Find the word that has the number code **6345**.

A ROLE   B LORE   C FLEE   D LURE   E FORE

The number codes for three of these four words are listed in a random order.
Work out the code to answer the questions.

TIME   RATE   TEEM   MEET

3662   5436   3126

58 Find the code for the word **RATE**.

A 5413   B 6214   C 5243   D 6241   E 5436

59 Find the code for the word **MERE**.

A 5343   B 2656   C 6515   D 2151   E 1636

60 Find the word that has the number code **3512**.

A TREE   B RIME   C TRAM   D TRIM   E RITE

Find **two** words, one from each set of brackets, that are **closest** in meaning.
Mark **both** words on the answer sheet.

Example   (useless still hushed)   (motionless lazy idle)

                A useless   **X** motionless

                B still   **Y** lazy

                C hushed   **Z** idle

Answer   **still** and **motionless**

61 (determine assert prove)   (validate outline accept)

    A determine   **X** validate

    B assert   **Y** outline

    C prove   **Z** accept

62 (stranded detained located)   (forgotten marooned expelled)

    A stranded   **X** forgotten

    B detained   **Y** marooned

    C located   **Z** expelled

63 (expedition saga feat)   (edition story essay)

    A expedition   **X** edition

    B saga   **Y** story

    C feat   **Z** essay

64 (entitled deprived reimbursed)   (permitted awarded equipped)

    A entitled   **X** permitted

    B deprived   **Y** awarded

    C reimbursed   **Z** equipped

65 (possible flexible prone)   (favourable impressionable liable)

    A possible   **X** favourable

    B flexible   **Y** impressionable

    C prone   **Z** liable

Turn over to the next page

Find the letter that will finish the first word and start the second word of each pair.
The same letter must be used for both pairs.

Example   dar (?) ap   edi (?) alk

         A e   **B** l   **C** m   **D** t   **E** w

Answer   t

66   dat (?) nd   sof (?) im

       A o   **B** e   **C** d   **D** a   **E** t

67   roa (?) ug   char (?) ane

       A b   **B** t   **C** r   **D** m   **E** n

68   rin (?) ig   stin (?) et

       A d   **B** k   **C** g   **D** t   **E** b

69   mai (?) ush   foa (?) ed

       A m   **B** r   **C** l   **D** d   **E** p

70   chi (?) ue   toxi (?) ot

       A c   **B** n   **C** d   **D** h   **E** p

Find the word that has a similar meaning to the words in both sets of brackets.

Example   (blaze flame) (scorch char)

         A fire   **B** flare   **C** burn   **D** toast   **E** furnace

Answer   burn

71   (discuss consult) (grant bestow)

       A debate   **B** confer   **C** award   **D** review   **E** donate

72   (method mode) (intends plans)

       A calculates   **B** ways   **C** tactics   **D** means   **E** attempts

73   (ponder consider) (intentional meant)

       A evaluate   **B** muse   **C** design   **D** wilful   **E** deliberate

74 (different unalike) (clear plain)

    A distinct   **B** simple   **C** unique   **D** obvious   **E** discrete

75 (observe watch) (respect approval)

    A view   **B** honour   **C** regard   **D** esteem   **E** behold

---

Find the missing number to complete each sum.

Example $2 \times 6 = 3 \times (?)$

    A 2   **B** 3   **C** 4   **D** 6   **E** 8

Answer   **4**

76 $4 \times 3 = 8 + (?)$

    A 1   **B** 2   **C** 3   **D** 4   **E** 5

77 $24 \div 4 = 25 - (?)$

    A 5   **B** 6   **C** 13   **D** 19   **E** 20

78 $6 \times 3 + 5 = 22 + (?)$

    A 1   **B** 2   **C** 8   **D** 15   **E** 26

79 $70 \div 7 + 3 = 5 + (?)$

    A 2   **B** 4   **C** 8   **D** 13   **E** 16

80 $9 \times 2 + 8 = 19 + (?)$

    A 1   **B** 5   **C** 7   **D** 12   **E** 15

End of test

Glossary

adjective	A word that <u>describes</u> a <u>noun</u>, e.g. '<u>beautiful</u> morning', '<u>frosty</u> lawn'.
adverb	A word that <u>describes</u> a <u>verb</u> or an <u>adjective</u>, which often ends with the <u>suffix</u> '<u>-ly</u>', e.g. 'She laughed <u>happily</u>.', 'He ran <u>quickly</u>.'
anagram	When the <u>letters</u> in a word are <u>mixed up</u>, e.g. <u>SWE</u> is an anagram of <u>SEW</u>.
antonym	A word that has the <u>opposite meaning</u> to another, e.g. the antonym of 'good' is 'bad'.
compound word	A word that is made up of <u>two separate words</u>, e.g. 'coast' + 'guard' — '<u>coastguard</u>'.
consonants	The <u>21 letters</u> of the alphabet that <u>aren't vowels</u>.
factor	A number you can <u>divide</u> another number by to get a <u>whole number</u>, e.g. <u>2</u> is a factor of <u>6</u>, because 6 ÷ 2 = 3.
Fibonacci sequence	A <u>number sequence</u> where the <u>two previous numbers</u> are <u>added together</u> to give the <u>next number</u> in the sequence, e.g. 1, 2, 3, 5, 8, 13.
homographs	Words that are spelt the same but have <u>different meanings</u>, e.g. 'I want to <u>play</u>.' and 'I saw a <u>play</u>.'
mirror pair	A <u>pair of letters</u> that are an <u>equal distance</u> from the <u>middle</u> of the alphabet in <u>opposite directions</u>, e.g. '<u>L</u>' and '<u>O</u>', '<u>H</u>' and '<u>S</u>'.
multiple	The number you get when you <u>multiply</u> a <u>whole number</u> by another <u>whole number</u>.
multiple choice	A type of <u>11+ test</u> that gives you <u>answers</u> to choose from for <u>each question</u>.
noun	A word that <u>names</u> something, e.g. '<u>Paul</u>', '<u>cat</u>', '<u>fear</u>', '<u>childhood</u>'.
prefix	A string of letters that can be put <u>in front</u> of a word to <u>change its meaning</u>, e.g. '<u>un-</u>' can be added to '<u>lock</u>' to make '<u>unlock</u>'.
prime number	A number that can only be divided by <u>1</u> and <u>itself</u> to give a <u>whole number</u>, e.g. <u>7</u> can only be <u>divided</u> by 1 and 7.
square number	The number that is made when a number is <u>multiplied</u> by <u>itself</u>, e.g. 3 × 3 = 9, so <u>9</u> is a <u>square number</u>.
standard answer	A type of <u>11+ test</u> that asks you to <u>pick an answer</u> from several options for some questions, and write your <u>own</u> answer for others.
suffix	A string of letters that can be put <u>after</u> a word to <u>change its meaning</u>, e.g. '<u>-er</u>' can be added to the end of '<u>play</u>' to make '<u>player</u>'.
synonym	A word with a <u>similar meaning</u> to another word, e.g. '<u>big</u>' is a synonym of '<u>huge</u>'.
verb	An <u>action</u> or <u>doing</u> word, e.g. '<u>run</u>', '<u>went</u>', '<u>think</u>'.
vowels	The letters '<u>a</u>', '<u>e</u>', '<u>i</u>', '<u>o</u>' and '<u>u</u>'.

Answers

Section One — The Alphabet

Pages 4-5 — Alphabet Positions

1 a) **H** — H is at position 8 in the alphabet.
   b) **L** — L is at position 12 in the alphabet.
   c) **P** — P is at position 16 in the alphabet.
   d) **V** — V is at position 22 in the alphabet.

2 a) **R** — R would be at position 9.
   b) **M** — M would be at position 14.
   c) **G** — G would be at position 20.
   d) **C** — C would be at position 24.

3 a) **14**
   The middle letter is N, which is at position 14 in the alphabet.
   b) **15**
   The middle letter is O, which is at position 15 in the alphabet.
   c) **2**
   The middle letter is B, which is at position 2 in the alphabet.

4 **T**
   T would be at position 12.

5 **Z**
   Z would be at position 20.

Pages 6-7 — Identify a Letter From a Clue

1 a) **O**
   O is the letter that occurs most often in NOTORIOUS.
   b) **R**
   R is the letter that occurs most often in FEBRUARY.
   c) **S**
   S is the letter that occurs most often in SHIPMENTS.

2 a) **L**
   L is the only letter that occurs twice in SHALLOW.
   b) **N**
   N is the only letter that occurs twice in RESPLENDENT.
   c) **F**
   F is the only letter that occurs twice in HANDCUFFS.

3 **E**
   E is the only letter that occurs twice in DEADEN, once in DANCER, and once in DANDELION.

Pages 8-9 — Alphabetical Order

1 **confront**
   The words go in the order — 'conference', 'confides', 'confine', 'confront', 'confuse'.

2 **deliberate**
   The words go in the order — 'complicate', 'inmate', 'deliberate', 'irate', 'frustrate'.

Pages 10-11 — Practice Questions

1 a) **G** — G is at position 7 in the alphabet.
   b) **J** — J is at position 10 in the alphabet.
   c) **S** — S is at position 19 in the alphabet.
   d) **X** — X is at position 24 in the alphabet.

2 a) **U** — U would be at position 6 in the alphabet.
   b) **O** — O would be at position 12 in the alphabet.
   c) **J** — J would be at position 17 in the alphabet.
   d) **E** — E would be at position 22 in the alphabet.

3 a) **4** — D is at position 4 in the alphabet.
   b) **18** — R is at position 18 in the alphabet.
   c) **12** — L is at position 12 in the alphabet.
   d) **16** — P is at position 16 in the alphabet.

4 a) **6**
   F is the middle letter and it is at position 6 in the alphabet.
   b) **23**
   W is the middle letter and it is at position 23 in the alphabet.
   c) **11**
   K is the middle letter and it is at position 11 in the alphabet.
   d) **15**
   O is the middle letter and it is at position 15 in the alphabet.

5 **K**
   K would be at position 6.

6 **W**
   W would be at position 16.

7 **11**
   N would be at position 11.

8 **19**
   V would be at position 19.

9 **12**
   R would be at position 12.

10 **R**
   R is the only letter that occurs once in STRATEGY and twice in REABSORB.

11 **N**
   N is the letter that occurs most often in ANCIENT, ANTENNA and ANNOYING.

12 **L**
   L is the only letter that occurs once in GALACTIC and once in GRIDLOCK, but not in GRASPING.

13 **O**
   O is the only letter that occurs once in SUPERPOWERS, once in RENOUNCED and twice in ACCOMMODATE.

14 a) **merriment**
   The words go in the order 'meadows', 'medieval', 'melody', 'merriment'.
   b) **prevail**
   The words go in the order 'precipice', 'prefaced', 'prepped', 'prevail'.
   c) **tantrum**
   The words go in the order 'tangible', 'tangled', 'tantalise', 'tantrum'.

15 a) **entertaining**
   The words go in the order 'sightseeing', 'entertaining', 'prizewinning', 'everlasting'.
   b) **authenticity**
   The words go in the order 'eccentricity', 'authenticity', 'invincibility', 'tranquillity'.
   c) **unintended**
   The words go in the order 'barricaded', 'unintended', 'rescinded', 'absentminded'.

Section Two — Making Words

Pages 12-13 — Preparing for the Test

1 a) **Answers may vary**
   Various answers possible, e.g. 'stroke', 'string', 'strict', 'stripe'.
   b) **No**
   There are no words in English which begin with 'blr'.
   c) **Answers may vary**
   Various answers possible, e.g. 'shrink', 'shrub', 'shrug', 'shrine'.
   d) **No**
   There are no words in English which begin with 'ds'.

2 a) **CRAZY**
   The unscrambled word is CRAZY.
   b) **MIXING**
   The unscrambled word is MIXING.
   c) **PLACEMENT**
   The unscrambled word is PLACEMENT.

Pages 14-15 — Missing Letters

1 a) **f**
The new words are 'calf' and 'flap'.

   b) **y**
The new words are 'toy' and 'you'.

   c) **e**
The new words are 'toe' and 'elf'.

   d) **m**
The new words are 'slim' and 'mix'.

2 a) **g**
The new words are 'dog', 'gap', 'plug' and 'gram'.

   b) **s**
The new words are 'was', 'soon', 'miss' and 'sun'.

Pages 16-17 — Move a Letter

1 **l**
The new words are 'cone' and 'glad'.

2 **p**
The new words are 'slit' and 'peel'.

3 **p**
The new words are 'ride' and 'pair'.

4 **r**
The new words are 'cook' and 'crow'.

5 **e**
The new words are 'clan' and 'cape'.

6 **w**
The new words are 'heat' and 'swell'.

Pages 18-19 — Hidden Word

1 **peat**
The word is hidden across the words 'turnip eaten'.

2 **cake**
The word is hidden across the words 'Rebecca keeps'.

3 **sofa**
The word is hidden across the words 'also farms'.

4 **idol**
The word is hidden across the words 'placid old'.

5 **joke**
The word is hidden across the words 'banjo keeps'.

6 **inch**
The word is hidden across the words 'in cheese'.

Pages 20-21 — Find the Missing Word

1 **ROW**
The complete word is FROWNED.

2 **IMP**
The complete word is GLIMPSED.

Pages 22-23 — Use a Rule to Make a Word

1 **nib**
Take letter 3 from the first word, followed by letters 2 and 3 from the second word.

2 **asp**
Take letter 3 from the second word, followed by letters 1 and 2 from the first word.

3 **seat**
Take letter 1 from the second word, followed by letter 2 from the first word, then letter 3 from the second word, then letter 4 from the first word.

4 **pail**
Take letter 3 from the second word, followed by letter 2 from the first word, then letter 2 from the second word, then letter 4 from the first word.

Pages 24-25 — Compound Words

1 **rotten**
'rotten' is the only correctly spelled word that can be made.

2 **beware**
'beware' is the only correctly spelled word that can be made.

3 **dragon**
'dragon' is the only correctly spelled word that can be made.

4 **clothe**
'clothe' is the only correctly spelled word that can be made.

Pages 26-27 — Complete a Word Pair

1 **able**
Remove letters 1 and 6, leaving the remaining letters in the order 2, 3, 4, 5.

2 **oat**
Rearrange letters 2, 3, 5 in the order 5, 2, 3.

3 **sat**
Rearrange letters 2, 3, 6 in the order 6, 2, 3.

4 **rat**
Rearrange letters 2, 3, 7 in the order 7, 2, 3.

Pages 28-29 — Anagram in a Sentence

1 **NEPHEWS**
NEPHEWS is the only correctly spelled word that fits the sentence.

2 **CLOUDY**
CLOUDY is the only correctly spelled word that fits the sentence.

3 **LASAGNE**
LASAGNE is the only correctly spelled word that fits the sentence.

4 **CAREFULLY**
CAREFULLY is the only correctly spelled word that fits the sentence.

5 **SHINGLE**
SHINGLE is the only correctly spelled word that fits the sentence.

Page 30 — Word Ladders

1 **(SLED) (FLED)**
The ladder is — SPED (SLED) (FLED) FLEA.

2 **(BASE) (BASS)**
The ladder is — CASE (BASE) (BASS) BOSS.

Pages 31-38 — Practice Questions

1 **h**
The new words are 'wish', 'hay', 'forth' and 'hone'.

2 **n**
The new words are 'span', 'nods', 'mean' and 'noun'.

3 **w**
The new words are 'shrew', 'wisp', 'stew' and 'way'.

4 **e**
The new words are 'shore', 'eats', 'ache' and 'earn'.

5 **p**
The new words are 'step', 'pear', 'steep' and 'pace'.

6 **e**
The new words are 'care', 'ewes', 'gape' and 'ear'.

7 **k**
The new words are 'husk', 'kerb', 'seek' and 'kept'.

8 **d**
The new words are 'herd', 'day', 'weld' and 'dire'.

9 **t**
The new words are 'slot', 'tide', 'get' and 'toil'.

10 **n**
The new words are 'been', 'nail', 'then' and 'nine'.

11 **g**
The new words are 'rag', 'gave', 'snug' and 'gasp'.

12 **l**
The new words are 'heal', 'lend', 'coal' and 'leek'.

13 **i**
The new words are 'deal' and 'said'.

14 **l**
The new words are 'band' and 'plot'.

15 **k**
The new words are 'lied' and 'pink'.

16 n
The new words are 'toes' and 'many'.

17 u
The new words are 'moth' and 'menu'.

18 m
The new words are 'ties' and 'form'.

19 r
The new words are 'fist' and 'iron'.

20 l
The new words are 'spit' and 'rule'.

21 n
The new words are 'beds' and 'hand'.

22 g
The new words are 'lobe' and 'sung'.

23 r
The new words are 'dawn' and 'rare'.

24 i
The new words are 'fled' and 'pain'.

25 wardrobe anywhere
The hidden word is 'bean'.

26 numb ankle
The hidden word is 'bank'.

27 turtle another
The hidden word is 'lean'.

28 to reveal
The hidden word is 'tore'.

29 both used
The hidden word is 'thus'.

30 banjo in
The hidden word is 'join'.

31 watermelon grew
The hidden word is 'long'.

32 swap lottery
The hidden word is 'plot'.

33 pupil each
The hidden word is 'pile'.

34 consider entering
The hidden word is 'rent'.

35 Grandpa gets
The hidden word is 'page'.

36 bacon lying
The hidden word is 'only'.

37 RAN
The complete word is ARRANGE.

38 PIT
The complete word is DESPITE.

39 LAP
The complete word is COLLAPSED.

40 BAT
The complete word is DEBATES.

41 DIG
The complete word is INDIGNANT.

42 DUE
The complete word is SUBDUED.

43 GET
The complete word is FIDGETS.

44 PAT
The complete word is SYMPATHY.

45 LAW
The complete word is CLAWING.

46 OIL
The complete word is RECOILED.

47 ALL
The complete word is GALLERY.

48 RAM
The complete word is TRAMPLE.

49 look
Take letter 2 from the first word, followed by letter 2 from the second word, followed by letter 4 from the first word, and then letter 4 from the second word.

50 belt
Take letter 4 from the first word, followed by letter 4 from the second word, followed by letter 2 from the first word, and then letter 3 from the second word.

51 idle
Take letter 2 from the first word, followed by letter 3 from the second word, followed by letter 1 from the first word, and then letter 2 from the second word.

52 nice
Take letter 4 from the second word, followed by letter 1 from the first word, followed by letter 3 from the first word, and then letter 1 from the second word.

53 cap
Take letter 1 from the first word, followed by letter 1 from the second word, and then letter 2 from the second word.

54 task
Take letter 4 from the first word, followed by letter 3 from the first word, followed by letter 1 from the second word, and then letter 4 from the second word.

55 rent
Take letter 1 from the first word, followed by letter 2 from the first word, followed by letter 4 from the second word, and then letter 1 from the second word.

56 one
Take letter 3 from the first word, followed by letter 2 from the second word, and then letter 2 from the first word.

57 bear
Take letter 2 from the second word, followed by letter 3 from the first word, followed by letter 1 from the second word, and then letter 4 from the first word.

58 tent
Take letter 3 from the second word, followed by letter 2 from the second word, followed by letter 2 from the first word, and then letter 3 from the first word.

59 hero
Take letter 4 from the second word, followed by letter 4 from the first word, followed by letter 1 from the second word, and then letter 1 from the first word.

60 nest
Take letter 3 from the first word, followed by letter 2 from the first word, followed by letter 1 from the second word, and then letter 4 from the first word.

61 uplift
'uplift' is the only correctly spelled word that can be made.

62 overgrown
'overgrown' is the only correctly spelled word that can be made.

63 anymore
'anymore' is the only correctly spelled word that can be made.

64 discover
'discover' is the only correctly spelled word that can be made.

65 wasteland
'wasteland' is the only correctly spelled word that can be made.

66 forage
'forage' is the only correctly spelled word that can be made.

67 behave
'behave' is the only correctly spelled word that can be made.

68 notice
'notice' is the only correctly spelled word that can be made.

69 lifelike
'lifelike' is the only correctly spelled word that can be made.

70 moreover
'moreover' is the only correctly spelled word that can be made.

71 before
'before' is the only correctly spelled word that can be made.

72 timeline
'timeline' is the only correctly spelled word that can be made.

73 far
Remove letters 3, 4, 5 and 7, leaving the remaining letters in the order 1, 2, 6.

74 hit
Remove letters 2, 3, 5 and 6, leaving the remaining letters in the order 1, 4, 7.

75 our
Rearrange letters 2, 3, 5 in the order 5, 2, 3.

76 long
Remove letters 3 and 4, leaving the remaining letters in the order 1, 2, 5, 6.

77 stop
Rearrange letters 1, 2, 3 and 4 in the order 4, 3, 2, 1.

78 roar
Rearrange letters 2, 3, 4 and 5 in the order 4, 5, 2, 3.

79 once
Remove letters 1 and 3, leaving the remaining letters in the order 2, 4, 5, 6.

80 bite
Rearrange letters 1, 5, 6 and 7 in the order 5, 6, 7, 1.

81 red
Remove letters 1, 2, 3, and 5, leaving the remaining letters in the order 4, 6, 7.

82 rat
Remove letters 1 and 4, leaving the remaining letters in the order 2, 3, 5.

83 tide
Rearrange letters 1, 2, 3 and 4 in the order 4, 3, 2, 1.

84 gear
The first letter of the word moves forward five places along the alphabet.

85 IMPULSE
IMPULSE is the only correctly spelled word that fits the sentence.

86 CENTRE
CENTRE is the only correctly spelled word that fits the sentence.

87 MUSCLES
MUSCLES is the only correctly spelled word that fits the sentence.

88 HORIZON
HORIZON is the only correctly spelled word that fits the sentence.

89 AMBITION
AMBITION is the only correctly spelled word that fits the sentence.

90 FOREIGN
FOREIGN is the only correctly spelled word that fits the sentence.

91 HINDERED
HINDERED is the only correctly spelled word that fits the sentence.

92 PRIVILEGE
PRIVILEGE is the only correctly spelled word that fits the sentence.

93 SINCERELY
SINCERELY is the only correctly spelled word that fits the sentence.

94 ASSUMED
ASSUMED is the only correctly spelled word that fits the sentence.

95 MINUTE
MINUTE is the only correctly spelled word that fits the sentence.

96 BROWSED
BROWSED is the only correctly spelled word that fits the sentence.

Section Three — Word Meanings
Pages 39-40 — Preparing for the Test

1 a) verb
'sang' is a verb because it is a doing word.

b) noun
'honesty' is an abstract noun because you can't touch, taste, smell, feel or hear it.

c) adjective
'nosy' is an adjective because it can be used to describe a noun.

d) verb
'tighten' is a verb because it is a doing word.

e) adjective
'cryptic' is an adjective because it can be used to describe a noun.

f) verb & noun
'play' is a verb because it is a doing word. It's also a noun because it is the name of an object or thing.

g) adverb
'vacantly' is an adverb because it describes a verb.

h) noun
'talent' is an abstract noun because you can't touch, taste, smell, feel or hear it.

2 a) noun
'truth' is an abstract noun that means 'the reality of a matter'.

b) adjective
'cantankerous' is an adjective that means 'grumpy' or 'disagreeable'.

c) adjective
'wrathfully' is an adverb that means 'angrily'.

d) noun
'bemusement' is a noun that means 'confusion'.

Pages 41-43 — Closest Meaning

1 afraid terrified
Both of these mean 'to be very scared'.

2 trail track
Both of these mean 'a path' or 'to follow something'.

3 smiled beamed
Both of these mean 'to grin broadly'.

Pages 44-46 — Opposite Meaning

1 absent present
'absent' means 'away', whereas 'present' means 'here'.

2 accuse defend
'accuse' means 'to blame someone', whereas 'defend' means 'to keep someone safe' or 'to argue someone's case'.

3 abolish establish
'abolish' means 'to end something', whereas 'establish' means 'to start something'.

Pages 47-49 — Multiple Meanings

1 talk
'talk' can mean 'a presentation' or 'to converse'.

2 run
'run' can mean 'to be in charge' or 'to move quickly'.

3 book
'book' can mean 'to arrange something' or 'something you read'.

Pages 50-51 — Odd Ones Out

1 calm peaceful
The other three all mean 'boring'.

2 poem novel
The other three are non-fiction texts.

3 slumbering dormant
The other three all mean 'to feel tired'.

Pages 52-54 — Word Connections

1 shell coat
They are the outer coverings of lobsters and dogs.

2 scissors telescope
They are the objects that cut and magnify.

3 unlucky bald
They are the opposites of 'fortunate' and 'hairy'.

Pages 55-56 — Reorder Words to Make a Sentence

1 **Quickly   take**
The sentence is 'Take the footpath if you want to get there quickly'.

2 **Fluffy   Nan**
The sentence is 'My Nan has a pet Beagle called Fluffy'.

3 **bolts   robot**
The sentence is 'The robot had silver bolts and blue wires'.

4 **week   a**
The sentence is 'It's my birthday a week today'.

Pages 57-62 — Practice Questions

1 **clasp   clutch**
Both of these mean 'to grip tightly'.

2 **relentless   continuous**
Both of these mean 'without end'.

3 **counter   oppose**
Both of these mean 'to argue against'.

4 **style   technique**
Both of these mean 'a way of doing something'.

5 **range   extent**
Both of these mean 'the area covered by something'.

6 **delay   detain**
Both of these mean 'to hold someone or something back'.

7 **crouch   stoop**
Both of these mean 'to duck down'.

8 **detailed   exhaustive**
Both of these mean 'thorough'.

9 **particle   granule**
Both of these mean 'a small piece of something'.

10 **forward   bold**
Both of these mean 'overfamiliar in social situations'.

11 **withdraw   retract**
Both of these mean 'to take something back'.

12 **linger   loiter**
Both of these mean 'to wait around aimlessly'.

13 **expose   conceal**
'expose' means 'to reveal', whereas 'conceal' means 'to cover up'.

14 **approach   recede**
'approach' means 'to go towards', whereas
'recede' means 'to move away from'.

15 **conflict   harmony**
'conflict' means 'disagreement', whereas 'harmony' means 'agreement'.

16 **unusual   routine**
'unusual' means 'not ordinary', whereas 'routine' means 'ordinary'.

17 **flushed   ashen**
'flushed' means 'having red and hot skin', whereas
'ashen' means 'having very pale skin'.

18 **overjoyed   devastated**
'overjoyed' means 'extremely happy', whereas
'devastated' means 'extremely sad'.

19 **ally   adversary**
'ally' means 'someone who cooperates with someone else', whereas
'adversary' means 'someone who works against someone else'.

20 **inessential   imperative**
'inessential' means 'not crucial', whereas 'imperative' means 'crucial'.

21 **uncommon   prevalent**
'uncommon' means 'not common', whereas
'prevalent' means 'widespread'.

22 **premature   overdue**
'premature' means 'early', whereas 'overdue' means 'late.'

23 **encourage   dispirit**
'encourage' means 'to give support or confidence to someone',
whereas 'dispirit' means 'to cause someone to lose confidence'.

24 **current   obsolete**
'current' means 'something that exists or is used now', whereas
'obsolete' means 'something that is no longer used'.

25 **school**
'school' can mean 'a place where students are educated' or 'to teach'.

26 **confront**
'confront' can mean 'to question the validity of something'
or 'to deal with something'.

27 **whisper**
'whisper' can mean 'a hint of something' or 'to speak quietly'.

28 **light**
'light' can mean 'very bright' or 'to set something on fire'.

29 **bother**
'bother' can mean 'effort caused by carrying out
an inconvenient task' or 'to irritate'.

30 **clouded**
'clouded' can mean 'made less clear' or 'dark and gloomy'.

31 **missing**
'missing' can mean 'not having something that
you need or want' or 'unable to be found'.

32 **offer**
'offer' can mean 'to supply' or 'to present to someone'.

33 **pen**
'pen' can mean 'a place where animals are kept' or
'to write something'.

34 **wonder**
'wonder' can mean 'an amazing thing' or 'a
feeling or state of amazement'.

35 **merit**
'merit' can mean 'to be worthy of something' or
'a praiseworthy quality'.

36 **build**
'build' can mean 'to construct something' or
'the shape of someone's body'.

37 **subordinate   counterpart**
The other three are positions of leadership.

38 **lifting   hurdle**
The other three refer to a sudden increase.

39 **complain   blame**
The other three mean 'to express grief'.

40 **remedy   therapy**
The other three are words associated with illness.

41 **speciality   talent**
The other three mean 'self-control'.

42 **shred   morsel**
The other three mean 'a large piece of something'.

43 **defeat   vanquish**
The other three mean 'to cause disgust or revulsion'.

44 **barren   yielding**
The other three are used to describe something
that is useless or ineffective.

45 **hushed   discreet**
The other three mean 'not spoken'.

46 **graze   chafe**
The other three mean 'to make a cut or opening in something'.

47 **professional   judgement**
The other three mean 'skill'.

48 **resistance   timidity**
The other three mean 'worry'.

49 **window   door**
They are the things that have panes and panels.

50 **past   current**
They are synonyms of 'historical' and 'modern'.

51 **shallow   restricted**
They are antonyms of 'deep' and 'expansive'.

52 **map   microscope**
They are pieces of equipment used by navigators and scientists.

53 **tree   bush**
They are what pears and gooseberries grow on.

54 fire ocean
They are things that are amber and turquoise in colour.

55 food knowledge
They are things you get if you forage and learn.

56 flourish shrivel
They are synonyms of 'bloom' and 'wither'.

57 memory success
They are the things that can cause feelings of nostalgia and satisfaction.

58 affordable destitute
They are antonyms of 'expensive' and 'rich'.

59 house hotel
They are the buildings where halls and lobbies are found.

60 skin rind
They are the outer layer of potatoes and oranges.

61 inside happily
The words can be rearranged into the sentence
'The experienced astronaut happily floats inside her spaceship.'

62 every dedicated
The words can be rearranged into the sentence
'The dedicated athletes run ten miles every other day.'

63 bouquet gave
The words can be rearranged into the sentence
'She generously gave me a beautiful bouquet of flowers.'

64 one going
The words can be rearranged into the sentence
'I am definitely going to travel around the world one day.'

65 in step-sister
The words can be rearranged into the sentence
'My oldest step-sister is a respected soldier in the army.'

66 fluently can
The words can be rearranged into the sentence
'Mateo can speak both Spanish and English fluently.'

67 the car
The words can be rearranged into the sentence
'Our rusty car broke down at the side of the motorway.'

68 were when
The words can be rearranged into the sentence
'I went skydiving when we were holidaying in Thailand last year.'

69 along curious
The words can be rearranged into the sentence
'The curious rat scampered along the empty street at night.'

70 second almost
The words can be rearranged into the sentence
'Kalifa has almost finished writing her second fantasy novel.'

71 tonight planning
The words can be rearranged into the sentence
'He is planning to bake a giant chocolate cake later tonight.'

72 tripped exclaimed
The words can be rearranged into the sentence
'Joe exclaimed when he suddenly tripped over the protruding rock.'

Section Four — Maths and Sequences

Pages 65-66 — Complete the Sum

1 20
$11 \times 4 = 44$, $44 = 24 + 20$

2 7
$30 - 4 = 26$, $26 = 19 + 7$

3 4
$54 \div 9 = 6$, $6 = 2 + 4$

4 6
$18 \div 3 \times 2 + 4 = 16$, $16 = 10 + 6$

Pages 67-69 — Letter Sequences

1 EY
The first letter moves forward 5 letters each time.
The second letter moves back 4 letters each time.

2 IS
The first letter moves in the sequence +1, 0, -1, -2, -3. The second letter moves forward two letters, then four letters alternately.

Pages 70-72 — Number Sequences

1 34
The numbers follow the sequence -4, -5, -4, -5.

2 43
Add even numbers in ascending order: +4, +6, +8, +10.

3 11
Subtract prime numbers in descending order: -11, -7, -5, -3.

4 3
Divide each number by 3 each time.

Pages 73-75 — Related Numbers

1 38
Add the two outer numbers.

2 31
Multiply the two outer numbers and then subtract 1.

3 8
Divide the third number by the first number and double the result.

4 22
Find the mid-point between the two outer numbers by adding the outer numbers together and dividing the answer by 2.

Pages 76-77 — Letter-Coded Sums

1 E
$7 \times 4 = 28$, E = 28

2 E
$11 \times 3 - 14 = 19$, E = 19

3 D
$45 \div 9 \times 3 = 15$, D = 15

4 A
$12 \times 4 - 17 - 27 = 4$, A = 4

Pages 78-82 — Practice Questions

1 6
$49 \div 7 = 7$, $7 = 1 + 6$

2 3
$9 + 3 = 12$, $12 = 36 \div 3$

3 9
$25 - 7 = 18$, $18 = 2 \times 9$

4 17
$14 \div 7 = 2$, $2 = 19 - 17$

5 3
$2 \times 11 + 14 = 36$, $36 = 39 - 3$

6 10
$21 \div 7 + 4 = 7$, $7 = 17 - 10$

7 1
$4 \times 8 + 14 = 46$, $46 = 45 + 1$

8 3
$90 \div 9 + 13 = 23$, $23 = 20 + 3$

9 12
$49 - 10 + 13 = 52$, $52 = 40 + 12$

10 11
$3 + 29 - 10 = 22$, $22 = 2 \times 11$

11 24
$42 \div 6 + 31 = 38$, $38 = 14 + 24$

12 12
$4 \times 9 + 7 = 43$, $43 = 31 + 12$

13 JT
The first letter in the pair moves in the sequence −1, +1.
The second letter moves in the sequence +1, −2.

14 TI
The first letter in the pair moves in the sequence −1, −2.
The second letter moves in the sequence +5, −1.

15 AB
The first letter in the pair moves in the sequence +3,–1.
The second letter moves in the sequence –4, –3.

16 NZ
The first letter in the pair moves forward 2 letters each time.
The second letter moves in the sequence +4, +3, +2, +1, 0.

17 TA
The first letter in each pair moves back 5 letters each time.
The second letter in each pair moves in the sequence +5, +4, +3, +2, +1.

18 TG
The first letter in the pair moves in the sequence +5, +1.
The second letter moves in the sequence +1, +3.

19 FE
The first letter in each pair moves in the sequence –1, 0, +1, +2, +3.
The second letter in each pair moves forward 4 letters each time.

20 MD
The first letter in each pair moves in the sequence +4, +2.
The second letter in each pair moves in the sequence –4, –3, –2, –1, 0.

21 UX
The first letter in each pair moves in the sequence
+1, 0, –1, –2, –3. The second letter in each pair moves
forward 3 letters and then back 4 letters.

22 AV
The first letter in each pair moves forward 5 letters each time.
The second letter in each pair moves in the sequence +2, +1, 0, –1, –2.

23 CO
The first letter in each pair moves back 1 letter each time.
The second letter in each pair moves in the sequence –1, –2, –3, –4, –5.

24 EC
The first letter in each pair moves back 1 letter and
then forward 4 letters. The second letter in each
pair moves in the sequence –2, –1, 0, +1, +2.

25 9
Subtract 8 each time.

26 1
Halve the numbers each time.

27 22
The number added decreases by 1 each time: +5, +4, +3, +2, +1.

28 17
There are two alternating sequences. For the first sequence, add
3 each time. For the second sequence, subtract 7 each time.

29 42
There are two alternating sequences. For the first sequence,
add 1 each time. For the second sequence, add 10 each time.

30 35
The number added decreases by 1 each time: +6, +5, +4, +3, +2.

31 29
The number added increases by 2 each time: +1, +3, +5, +7, +9.

32 42
The numbers follow the sequence –2, –1, 0, +1, +2.

33 35
The number added increases by 2 each time: +2, +4, +6, +8, +10.

34 4
There are two alternating sequences. For the first sequence,
subtract 7 each time. For the second sequence, add 4 each time.

35 24
There are two alternating sequences. For the first sequence, multiply
by 2 each time. For the second sequence, subtract 5 each time.

36 1
Divide by ascending numbers: ÷1, ÷2, ÷3, ÷4, ÷5

37 1
Divide the first number by the third number, then divide by 2.

38 9
Add the two outside numbers together, then subtract 4.

39 6
Subtract the third number from the first number,
then multiply by the third number.

40 12
Subtract the third number from the first number, then add 5.

41 9
Multiply the two outside numbers together, then divide by 2.

42 35
Multiply the two outside numbers together,
then subtract the third number.

43 40
Divide the first number by the third number, then multiply by 5.

44 4
Multiply the two outside numbers together, then subtract 8.

45 26
Add the two outside numbers together, then multiply by 2.

46 4
Add the two outside numbers together, then divide by 6.

47 11
Subtract the third number from the first number, then add 4.

48 12
Multiply the two outside numbers together,
then subtract the first number.

49 A
$21 - 9 + 4 - 15 = 1, A = 1$

50 C
$24 \div 4 + 2 = 8, C = 8$

51 E
$5 + 6 - 2 + 8 = 17, E = 17$

52 D
$10 \div 5 \times 1 + 6 = 8, D = 8$

53 E
$9 \times 2 + 11 = 29, E = 29$

54 E
$6 \times 3 + 9 - 13 = 14, E = 14$

55 B
$21 \div 3 + 8 - 9 = 6, B = 6$

56 E
$3 \times 10 + 8 - 13 = 25, E = 25$

57 C
$10 \times 2 + 1 - 13 = 8, C = 8$

58 C
$11 - 9 \times 21 - 28 = 14, C = 14$

59 A
$27 \div 9 + 15 - 13 = 5, A = 5$

60 B
$14 \times 2 + 3 - 29 = 2, B = 2$

Section Five — Logic and Coding

Pages 84-85 —Letter Connections

1 KP
The first letter in the pair moves forward 2 letters.
The second letter moves back 2 letters.

2 ZY
The first letter in the pair moves forward 4 letters.
The second letter moves back 4 letters.

3 TL
The first letter in the pair moves forward 1 letter.
The second letter moves forward 7 letters.

4 SP
These are mirror pairs. B and Y are a mirror pair, as are E and V.
The corresponding mirror pairs for H and K are S and P.

Pages 86-88 — Letter-Word Codes

1 KNL
To get from the word to the code, move each letter forward 5.

2 LOYAL
To get from the code to the word, move the
letters in the sequence -3, +3, -3, +3, -3.

3 DUMSM
To get from the word to the code, move the letters in the sequence +2, +3, +4, +5, +6.

Pages 89-90 — Number-Word Codes

1 3446
T = 3, O = 4, O = 4, L = 6

2 3451
T = 3, O = 4, R = 5, N = 1

3 ROLL
R = 5, O = 4, L = 6, L = 6

Pages 91-92 — Explore the Facts

1 Marta
Marta sees a pedestrian, a cat, a tractor and a cyclist.

Pages 93-95 — Solve the Riddle

1 E
Nathan beat Li, and Li beat Zach. Zach didn't come last, and he can't have come fourth, so Zach must have come third and Li must have come second.

Pages 98-105 — Practice Questions

1 FW
Each letter in the pair moves forward 4 letters.

2 OR
Each letter in the pair moves back 6 letters.

3 BY
The first letter in the pair moves back 6 letters.
The second letter in the pair moves forward 2 letters.

4 UB
DU and WF are mirror pairs, where the two letters are an equal distance from the centre of the alphabet. The answer will be the mirror pairs for F and Y, which are U and B.

5 GD
The first letter in the pair moves back 3 letters.
The second letter in the pair moves forward 3 letters.

6 JD
ZV and AE are mirror pairs, where the two letters are an equal distance from the centre of the alphabet. The answer will be the mirror pairs for Q and W, which are J and D.

7 VC
The first letter in the pair moves forward 1 letter.
The second letter in the pair moves back 2 letters.

8 GM
XO and CL are mirror pairs, where the two letters are an equal distance from the centre of the alphabet. The answer will be the mirror pairs for T and N, which are G and M.

9 CB
WP and DK are mirror pairs, where the two letters are an equal distance from the centre of the alphabet. The answer will be the mirror pairs for X and Y, which are C and B.

10 RI
The first letter in the pair moves back 6 letters.
The second letter in the pair moves forward 6 letters.

11 UJ
The first letter in the pair moves back 2 letters.
The second letter in the pair moves forward 4 letters.

12 ZN
HL and SO are mirror pairs, where the two letters are an equal distance from the centre of the alphabet. The answer will be the mirror pairs for A and M, which are Z and N.

13 QET
To get from the word to the code, move each letter forward 4.

14 UFWY
To get from the word to the code, move each letter forward 5.

15 FONT
To get from the code to the word, move the letters in the sequence −2, +1, −2, +1.

16 UCJJ
To get from the word to the code, move each letter back 2.

17 ANNOY
To get from the code to the word, move the letters in the sequence +1, 0, −1, −2, −3.

18 GLFI
This is a mirror code, where each letter is an equal distance from the centre of the alphabet. T is 7 letters forward from the centre, and G is 7 letters back; O is 2 letters forward, and L is 2 letters back; U is 8 letters forward and F is 8 letters back; R is 5 letters forward and I is 5 letters back.

19 HINGE
To get from the code to the word, move each letter forward 3.

20 QKQO
To get from the word to the code, move the letters in the sequence +1, +2, +3, +4.

21 LINED
This is a mirror code, where each letter is an equal distance from the centre of the alphabet. O is 2 letters forward from the centre, and L is 2 letters back; R is 5 letters forward and I is 5 letters back; M is 1 letter back and N is 1 letter forward; V is 9 letters forward, and E is 9 letters back; W is 10 letters forward, and D is 10 letters back.

22 GWVWD
To get from the word to the code, move the letters in the sequence +1, +2, +3, +4, +5.

23 AMASS
To get from the code to the word, move the letters in the sequence −3, +4, −3, +4, −3.

24 HBBWN
To get from the word to the code, move the letters in the sequence −1, −2, −3, −4, −5.

25 1245
A = 1, R = 2, M = 4, S = 5

26 2614
R = 2, O = 6, A = 1, M = 4

27 SOAR
S = 5, O = 6, A = 1, R = 2

28 3561
F = 3, L = 5, E = 6, A = 1

29 4155
H = 4, A = 1, L = 5, L = 5

30 FATE
F = 3, A = 1, T = 2, E = 6

31 2351
R = 2, O = 3, A = 5, D = 1

32 3265
O = 3, R = 2, C = 6, A = 5

33 CODE
C = 6, O = 3, D = 1, E = 4

34 3142
S = 3, A = 1, L = 4, T = 2

35 5132
E = 5, A = 1, S = 3, T = 2

36 BEST
B = 6, E = 5, S = 3, T = 2

37 4661
D = 4, E = 6, E = 6, M = 1

38 5236
G = 5, A = 2, L = 3, E = 6

39 LEAD
L = 3, E = 6, A = 2, D = 4

40 1423
L = 1, E = 4, A = 2, F = 3

41 **5214**
T = 5, A = 2, L = 1, E = 4

42 **FAST**
F = 3, A = 2, S = 6, T = 5

43 **3621**
C = 3, A = 6, P = 2, E = 1

44 **2654**
P = 2, A = 6, I = 5, N = 4

45 **CANE**
C = 3, A = 6, N = 4, E = 1

46 **Jorge**
Jorge has four toppings: tomato, onions, cheese and bacon.

47 **Uri**
Uri has only been to Manchester.

48 **Sona**
Sona does four hobbies: swimming, hockey, boxing and cycling.

49 **Bianca**
Bianca likes four genres: comedy, horror, romance and action.

50 **Shirley**
Shirley is only using two colours: white and blue.

51 **Ella**
Ella helps out in four rooms: the kitchen,
lounge, dining room and garage.

52 **Anders**
Anders brought five types of food: crisps, sandwiches,
sausage rolls, cookies and brownies.

53 **Victor**
Victor only bought two types of fruit: apples and peaches.

54 **A**
Luca collected the second highest number of shells, and
Jasper collected more shells than Luca. This means
that Jasper must have collected the most shells.

55 **E**
Li has two pets. Petra has twice as many pets as Li, which means
she has four. Maria has one fewer pet than Petra, so she has three.
Craig and Naomi both have the same number of pets as Maria, which
means they have three. This means Naomi has more pets than Li.

56 **B**
Ellie comes third. Anza doesn't come fourth but beats Orla, which
means Anza must come first or second. John beats Anza, which
means he must come first and Anza must come second. This means
Orla must come fourth or fifth, so she can't have beaten Ellie.

57 **E**
Luke got on the bus at 5.45. Anthony got on twenty minutes after
Luke, which means he got on at 6.05. Jessie got on ten minutes
after Anthony, which means she got on at 6.15. Luke got on the
bus half an hour before Summer, which means Summer got on at
6.15 too. This means Jessie and Summer got on at the same time.

58 **B**
There are six apples. Between them, Bella, Ray and Gemma
eat five apples. This means Denny can't have eaten two
apples and a pear, because there is only one apple left.

59 **D**
Rachel scored 75 marks, which was five marks more than
Ash. This means Ash scored 70. Ash scored fifteen marks
fewer than Thandi, so Thandi must have scored 85.

Mixed Practice Tests
Pages 106-108 — Test 1

1 **perpetual   momentary**
'perpetual' means 'occurring continuously', whereas
'momentary' means 'occurring very briefly'.'

2 **disobey   comply**
'disobey' means 'to go against orders',
whereas 'comply' means 'to obey'.

3 **inquisitive   uninterested**
'inquisitive' means 'curious', whereas
'uninterested' means 'not curious'.

4 **passionate   apathetic**
'passionate' means 'enthusiastic about something',
whereas 'apathetic' means 'showing no interest'.

5 **pitch   court**
They are the places where rugby and basketball are played.

6 **remain   vacate**
They are antonyms of 'depart' and 'occupy'.

7 **pod   shell**
They are the things that encase peas and eggs.

8 **plenty   shortage**
They are synonyms for 'abundance' and 'scarcity'.

9 **7**
30 + 12 = 42, 42 = 49 − 7

10 **6**
18 ÷ 2 = 9, 9 = 3 + 6

11 **1**
12 + 5 − 10 = 7, 7 = 8 − 1

12 **5**
8 × 4 + 14 = 46, 46 = 51 − 5

13 **6431**
M = 6, O = 4, A = 3, T = 1

14 **1465**
T = 1, O = 4, M = 6, E = 5

15 **THEM**
T = 1, H = 2, E = 5, M = 6

16 **theatre   exit**
The hidden word is 'tree'.

17 **glad   you**
The hidden word is 'lady'.

18 **bear   chased**
The hidden word is 'arch'.

19 **chef   aired**
The hidden word is 'fair'.

20 **Frank**
Frank only has one poster: a unicorn poster.

Pages 109-111 — Test 2

1 **OAR**
The complete word is BOARDED.

2 **RAG**
The complete word is FRAGILE.

3 **TEN**
The complete word is STENCILS.

4 **HER**
The complete word is ARCHERY.

5 **option   choice**
The other three refer to something
that is done on a regular basis.

6 **textbook   dictionary**
The other three are types of fictional writing.

7 **searing   ignited**
The other three mean 'giving off light'.

8 **nourished   satisfied**
The other three mean 'ate quickly'.

9 **10**
Subtract the third number from the
first number, then multiply by 2.

10 **3**
Add the two outside numbers together, then divide by 3.

11 **1**
Divide the first number by the third number, then subtract 3.

12 **5**
Subtract the third number from the first number, then multiply by 5.

13 grid
Rearrange letters 2, 3, 4, 5 in the order 5, 2, 3, 4.

14 reel
Rearrange letters 1, 2, 5, 6 in the order 6, 5, 2, 1.

15 ears
Remove letters 1, 3, and 5, leaving the remaining letters in the order 2, 4, 6, 7.

16 gate
Rearrange letters 2, 3, 4, 7 in the order 7, 3, 4, 2.

17 WX
The first letter in each pair moves forward 2 letters each time. The second letter in each pair moves in the sequence –1, –2, –3, –4, –5.

18 TN
The first letter in the pair moves in the sequence +1, +3.
The second letter moves in the sequence +3, –2.

19 YP
The first letter in each pair moves in the sequence +3, +2, +1, 0, –1.
The second letter in each pair moves forward 5 letters each time.

20 ZY
The first letter in the pair moves in the sequence +2, +4.
The second letter moves in the sequence –2, –1.

Pages 112-114 — Test 3

1 abnormal outlandish
Both of these mean 'strange'.

2 seize commandeer
Both of these mean 'to take control of'.

3 bewildering mystifying
Both of these mean 'difficult to understand'.

4 unnerve perturb
Both of these mean 'to cause upset or worry'.

5 t
The new words are 'lost', 'tip', 'seat' and 'task'.

6 b
The new words are 'curb', 'bore', 'stub' and 'ban'.

7 o
The new words are 'solo', 'owe', 'tempo' and 'oath'.

8 s
The new words are 'dries', 'seal', 'bias' and 'sigh'.

9 A
$2 \times 4 \div 8 = 1$, A = 1

10 D
$20 \div 5 + 10 = 14$, D = 14

11 C
$2 \times 3 + 15 – 13 = 8$, C = 8

12 E
$18 \div 6 \times 9 + 8 = 35$, E = 35

13 format
'format' is the only correctly spelled word that can be made.

14 howled
'howled' is the only correctly spelled word that can be made.

15 tireless
'tireless' is the only correctly spelled word that can be made.

16 wavered
'wavered' is the only correctly spelled word that can be made.

17 NVDU
To get from the word to the code, move the letters in the sequence +4, –5, +4, –5.

18 RMMVI
This is a mirror code, where each letter is an equal distance from the centre of the alphabet. I is 5 letters back from the centre, and R is five letters forward; N is 1 letter forward, and M is 1 letter back; E is 9 letters back, and V is 9 letters forward; R is 5 letters forward, and I is 5 letters back.

19 PIECE
To get from the code to the word, move the letters in the sequence –1, 0, +1, +2, +3.

20 B
Darcy has one more sibling than Teddy. Teddy has one brother and one sister, so Darcy must have three siblings. Max has more siblings than Darcy, so he must have at least four siblings.

Pages 115-117 — Test 4

1 rotten
'rotten' can mean 'dishonest and immoral' or 'mouldy and decayed'.

2 crush
'crush' can mean 'to compress' or 'a large group of people tightly packed together'.

3 serious
'serious' can mean 'earnest' or 'of great importance'.

4 remedy
'remedy' can mean 'a treatment for an illness' or 'to put something right'.

5 f
The new words are 'deer' and 'flaw'.

6 r
The new words are 'ally' and 'ever'.

7 d
The new words are 'fuse' and 'body'.

8 h
The new words are 'cart' and 'ship'.

9 91
The number added increases by 2 each time:
+2, +4, +6, +8, +10.

10 1
There are two alternating sequences. For the first sequence, subtract 6 each time. For the second sequence, add 10 each time.

11 30
The numbers follow the sequence +2, +1, 0, –1, –2.

12 8
There are two alternating sequences. For the first sequence, multiply by 2 each time. For the second sequence, subtract 4 each time.

13 drab
Take letter 1 from the second word, followed by letter 2 from the first word, followed by letter 3 from the second word, and then letter 4 from the first word.

14 aged
Take letter 3 from the second word, followed by letter 2 from the first word, followed by letter 5 from the first word, and then letter 4 from the second word.

15 paid
Take letter 2 from the second word, followed by letter 2 from the first word, followed by letter 3 from the second word, and then letter 1 from the first word.

16 spot
Take letter 1 from the second word, followed by letter 2 from the first word, followed by letter 3 from the first word, and then letter 4 from the second word.

17 KJ
The first letter in the pair moves back 5 letters.
The second letter in the pair moves forward 1 letter.

18 PQ
NA and MZ are mirror pairs, where the two letters are an equal distance from the centre of the alphabet. The answer will be the mirror pairs for K and J, which are P and Q.

19 GO
The first letter in the pair moves forward 1 letter.
The second letter in the pair moves back 3 letters.

20 HE
HQ and SJ are mirror pairs, where the two letters are an equal distance from the centre of the alphabet. The answer will be the mirror pairs for S and V, which are H and E.

Practice Papers

Pages 118-129 — Practice Paper 1

1 NIT
The complete word is REUNITED.

2 HAS
The complete word is AGHAST.

3 LIE
The complete word is REPLIES.

4 DOT
The complete word is ANTIDOTE.

5 OAT
The complete word is LOATHES.

6 crops shears
The other three are types of crop.

7 cotton fabric
The other three refer to body coverings of animals.

8 tend nurture
The other three all mean 'to gather in crops'.

9 trailer cart
The other three are vehicles that are powered by engines.

10 ridge hill
The other three describe depressions in a surface.

11 baffled bewildered
The other three all mean 'very shocked or distressed'.

12 please accept
The other three all mean 'to express admiration'.

13 VI
The first letter in the pair moves forward 3 letters.
The second letter in the pair moves back 1 letter.

14 OI
JM and QN are mirror pairs, where the two letters are an equal distance from the centre of the alphabet. The answer will be the mirror pairs for L and R, which are O and I.

15 KY
The first letter in the pair moves back 2 letters.
The second letter in the pair moves forward 5 letters.

16 PL
The first letter in the pair moves forward 1 letter.
The second letter in the pair moves back 6 letters.

17 TJ
IT and RJ are mirror pairs, where the two letters are an equal distance from the centre of the alphabet. The answer will be the mirror pairs for G and Q, which are T and J.

18 37
The two previous numbers are added together to get the next number in the sequence, i.e. 4 + 5 = 9, 5 + 9 = 14 etc.

19 20
The number subtracted increases by 2 each time: −1, −3, −5, −7, −9.

20 16
There are two alternating sequences. For the first sequence, multiply by 2 each time. For the second sequence, add 6 each time.

21 33
There are two alternating sequences. For the first sequence, add 8 each time. For the second sequence, subtract 1 each time.

22 58
The numbers follow the sequence −1, 0, +1, +2, +3.

23 1
There are two alternating sequences. For the first sequence, divide by 4 each time. For the second sequence, add 1 each time.

24 are
Rearrange letters 2, 4, 5 in the order 4, 5, 2.

25 sat
Rearrange letters 2, 3, 4 in the order 3, 2, 4.

26 grin
Rearrange letters 4, 5, 6, 7 in the order 7, 4, 5, 6.

27 tin
Rearrange letters 1, 2, 3 in the order 3, 1, 2.

28 bode
Remove letters 2, 4, and 7, leaving the remaining letters in the order 1, 3, 5, 6.

29 intake
'intake' is the only correctly spelled word that can be made.

30 undertone
'undertone' is the only correctly spelled word that can be made.

31 passage
'passage' is the only correctly spelled word that can be made.

32 pleasing
'pleasing' is the only correctly spelled word that can be made.

33 backlash
'backlash' is the only correctly spelled word that can be made.

34 concede deny
'concede' means 'to accept the validity of something', whereas 'deny' means 'to reject the validity of something'.

35 liberate detain
'liberate' means 'to set free', whereas 'detain' means 'to keep captive'.

36 active stagnant
'active' means 'energetic', whereas 'stagnant' means 'inactive'.

37 insensitivity tact
'insensitivity' means 'a lack of awareness of someone's feelings', whereas 'tact' means 'sensitivity towards the feelings of others'.

38 provoke appease
'provoke' means 'to anger', whereas 'appease' means 'to make less angry'.

39 LINK
To get from the code to the word, move each letter backward 5.

40 KZJD
To get from the word to the code, move the letters in the sequence −3, −1, −3, −1.

41 IVORX
This is a mirror code, where each letter is an equal distance from the centre of the alphabet. R is 5 letters forward from the centre, and I is 5 letters back; E is 9 letters back, and V is 9 letters forward; L is 2 letters back and O is 2 letters forward; I is 5 letters back and R is 5 letters forward; C is 11 letters back and X is 11 letters forward.

42 ALLOW
To get from the code to the word, move the letters in the sequence +4, −4, +4, −4, +4.

43 MKHW
To get from the word to the code, move the letters in the sequence +1, +2, +3, +4.

44 SONG
This is a mirror code, where each letter is an equal distance from the centre of the alphabet. H is 6 letters back from the centre, and S is 6 letters forward; L is 2 letters back and O is 2 letters forward; M is 1 letter back and N is 1 letter forward; T is 7 letters forward and G is 7 letters back.

45 TDLLN
To get from the word to the code, move the letters in the sequence 0, −1, −2, −3, −4.

46 Astrid
Astrid only buys one snack: crackers.
Everybody else buys two or three snacks.

47 Emma
Emma saw three sea creatures: a starfish, a clownfish and a stingray.

48 AT
The first letter in the pair moves in the sequence −2, +1.
The second letter moves in the sequence −2, +3.

49 ZJ
The first letter in the pair moves in the sequence −1, −2.
The second letter moves in the sequence −1, +2.

50 JC
The first letter in each pair moves forward 1 letter each time.
The second letter in each pair moves in the sequence +4, +3, +2, +1, 0.

51 HR
The first letter in each pair moves forward 3 letters and
then forward 5 letters alternately. The second letter in
each pair moves in the sequence +3, +2, +1, 0, –1.

52 DI
The first letter in the pair moves in the sequence +1, 0, –1, –2, –3.
The second letter moves back 2 letters and then back 4 letters alternately.

53 5351
R = 5, A = 3, R = 5, E = 1

54 5116
R = 5, E = 1, E = 1, F = 6

55 FIRE
F = 6, I = 2, R = 5, E = 1

56 1542
L = 1, A = 5, N = 4, E = 2

57 4256
N = 4, E = 2, A = 5, T = 6

58 LEAN
L = 1, E = 2, A = 5, N = 4

59 t
The new words are 'even' and 'newt'.

60 h
The new words are 'were' and 'ache'.

61 p
The new words are 'lead' and 'spun'.

62 b
The new words are 'gale' and 'bred'.

63 n
The new words are 'rage' and 'town'.

64 D
$3 \times 9 - 13 = 14$, D = 14

65 D
$2 \times 16 \div 4 = 8$, D = 8

66 B
$16 \div 4 + 10 - 9 = 5$, B = 5

67 E
$8 + 4 \div 3 + 11 = 15$, E = 15

68 C
$10 \times 2 + 20 \div 4 = 10$, C = 10

69 13
Add the two outside numbers together, then add 5.

70 1
Divide the first number by the third number, then subtract 3.

71 5
Multiply the two outside numbers together, then divide by 3.

72 7
Subtract the third number from the first number, then add 2.

73 3
Divide the first number by the third number, then subtract 6.

74 k
The new words are 'stink', 'kick', 'trek' and 'keep'.

75 r
The new words are 'user', 'rail', 'clear' and 'rust'.

76 d
The new words are 'dated', 'due', 'reed' and 'daze'.

77 y
The new words are 'sway', 'year', 'shiny' and 'yank'.

78 f
The new words are 'loaf', 'fin', 'golf' and 'fee'.

79 D
Polly's team got more points than Taylor's team, and Olga's
team got more points than Polly's team. Therefore, Olga's
team must have scored more points than Taylor's team.

80 E
Meena arrived 15 minutes before the start of the play, so she must
have arrived at 6.45pm. Camila arrived 45 minutes before this at
6pm. Albert arrived thirty minutes after Camila at 6.30pm. Lucy
arrived right after Albert, so she must have arrived after Camila.

Pages 130-141 — Practice Paper 2

1 JR
The first letter in each pair moves in the sequence +3, +2, +1, 0, –1.
The second letter moves forward 1 letter each time.

2 IO
The first letter in each pair moves forward 2 letters each time.
The second letter in each pair moves in the sequence –2, –1, 0, +1, +2.

3 PT
The first letter in each pair moves in the sequence –3, –2, –1, 0, +1.
The second letter in each pair moves back 2 letters each time.

4 IQ
The first letter in each pair moves back 3 letters and
then back 1 letter alternately. The second letter in each
pair moves in the sequence –5, –4, –3, –2, –1.

5 YM
The first letter in each pair moves in the sequence –4, –3, –2, –1, 0.
The second letter in each pair moves forward 1 additional
letter each time, i.e. +1, +2, +3, +4, +5.

6 stun
Take letter 1 from the first word, followed by letter 4
from the second word, followed by letter 2 from the
first word, and then letter 3 from the first word.

7 meal
Take letter 4 from the second word, followed by letter
2 from the second word, followed by letter 1 from the
first word, and then letter 3 from the second word.

8 rate
Take letter 5 from the second word, followed by letter
1 from the second word, followed by letter 5 from the
first word, and then letter 2 from the first word.

9 tale
Take letter 4 from the second word, followed by letter
3 from the second word, followed by letter 4 from the
first word, and then letter 2 from the second word.

10 used
Take letter 3 from the second word, followed by letter
4 from the first word, followed by letter 3 from the
first word, and then letter 1 from the first word.

11 improve degenerate
'improve' means 'to get better', whereas
'degenerate' means 'to get worse'.

12 noticeable imperceptible
'noticeable' means 'visible', whereas 'imperceptible' means 'invisible'.

13 destructive beneficial
'destructive' means 'negative', whereas 'beneficial' means 'positive'.

14 ignorance understanding
'ignorance' means 'a lack of knowledge or comprehension',
whereas 'understanding' means 'comprehension'.

15 honesty duplicity
'honesty' means 'truthfulness', whereas
'duplicity' means 'dishonesty'.

16 kitten doesn't
The hidden word is 'tend'.

17 from over
The hidden word is 'move'.

18 undo several
The hidden word is 'dose'.

19 note arrived
The hidden word is 'tear'.

20 violin every
The hidden word is 'line'.

21 channel several
The hidden word is 'else'.

22 b
The new words are 'read' and 'beat'.

23 v
The new words are 'sole' and 'dove'.

24 p
The new words are 'raid' and 'pour'.

25 r
The new words are 'bake' and 'trip'.

26 e
The new words are 'grip' and 'rage'.

27 habitable
'habitable' is the only correctly spelled word that can be made.

28 person
'person' is the only correctly spelled word that can be made.

29 betray
'betray' is the only correctly spelled word that can be made.

30 startled
'startled' is the only correctly spelled word that can be made.

31 impact
'impact' is the only correctly spelled word that can be made.

32 71
The number added increases by 2 each time:
$+5, +7, +9, +11, +13$.

33 31
There are two alternating sequences. For the first sequence, minus 8 each time. For the second sequence, divide by 4 each time.

34 64
There are two alternating sequences. For the first sequence, add 5 each time. For the second sequence, multiply by 3 each time.

35 24
The number added decreases by 1 each time:
$+5, +4, +3, +2, +1$.

36 28
There are two alternating sequences. For the first sequence, subtract 4 each time. For the second sequence, divide by 3 each time.

37 10
There are two alternating sequences. For the first sequence, add 2 each time. For the second sequence, multiply by 4 each time.

38 each
Rearrange letters 3, 4, 5, 6 in the order 6, 3, 4, 5.

39 tour
Rearrange letters 1, 2, 3, 4 in the order 4, 2, 3, 1.

40 legs
Rearrange letters 2, 3, 6, 7 in the order 3, 2, 6, 7.

41 lean
Rearrange letters 1, 2, 4, 5 in the order 4, 5, 1, 2.

42 near
Rearrange letters 2, 3, 5, 6 in the order 5, 6, 2, 3.

43 E
$5 \times 4 + 7 = 27$, $E = 27$

44 D
$5 + 16 \div 3 = 7$, $D = 7$

45 C
$40 \div 10 + 3 - 2 = 5$, $C = 5$

46 A
$20 \div 5 + 10 - 12 = 2$, $A = 2$

47 E
$5 \times 3 + 1 \div 2 = 8$, $E = 8$

48 Bella
Bella only has one topping: jam.

49 Jake
Jake competed in four events: the long jump, the relay race, the 100m sprint and the three-legged race.

50 pencil pen
They are the writing tools that contain lead and ink.

51 space ocean
They are the places where rockets and submarines are used for exploration and travel.

52 build destroy
They are antonyms for 'dismantle' and 'create'.

53 solidify melt
They are synonyms for 'freeze' and 'thaw'.

54 obedience rebellion
They are the actions that cause order and disorder.

55 4365
$R = 4, U = 3, L = 6, E = 5$

56 4221
$R = 4, O = 2, O = 2, F = 1$

57 LURE
$L = 6, U = 3, R = 4, E = 5$

58 5436
$R = 5, A = 4, T = 3, E = 6$

59 2656
$M = 2, E = 6, R = 5, E = 6$

60 TRIM
$T = 3, R = 5, I = 1, M = 2$

61 prove validate
Both of these mean 'to show that something is true'.

62 stranded marooned
Both of these mean 'left or trapped somewhere'.

63 saga story
Both of these can mean 'a long tale'.

64 entitled permitted
Both of these mean 'officially allowed to do something'.

65 prone liable
Both of these mean 'likely to do something'.

66 a
The new words are 'data', 'and', 'sofa' and 'aim'.

67 m
The new words are 'roam', 'mug', 'charm' and 'mane'.

68 g
The new words are 'ring', 'gig', 'sting' and 'get'.

69 l
The new words are 'mail', 'lush', 'foal' and 'led'.

70 c
The new words are 'chic', 'cue', 'toxic' and 'cot'.

71 confer
'confer' can mean 'to have discussions' or 'to give to'.

72 means
'means' can mean 'a way of doing something' or 'means to do'.

73 deliberate
'deliberate' can mean 'to think about' or 'on purpose'.

74 distinct
'distinct' can mean 'separate' or 'well-defined'.

75 regard
'regard' can mean 'to look at' or 'esteem'.

76 4
$4 \times 3 = 12$, $12 = 8 + 4$

77 19
$24 \div 4 = 6$, $6 = 25 - 19$

78 1
$6 \times 3 + 5 = 23$, $23 = 22 + 1$

79 8
$70 \div 7 + 3 = 13$, $13 = 5 + 8$

80 7
$9 \times 2 + 8 = 26$, $26 = 19 + 7$

Answers

Index